Quick & Easy
Home Sewing
Projects

50 Low- and No-sew Projects
to Enhance Every Room in Your Home

Gloria Nicol

Reader's
Digest

The Reader's Digest Association, Inc.
Pleasantville, New York/Montreal/London/Hong Kong

A READER'S DIGEST BOOK

This edition published by The Reader's Digest Association, Inc.
by arrangement with Cico Books

FOR CICO BOOKS
Photography: Gloria Nicol
Editor: Sarah Hoggett
Illustrations: Kate Simunek
Design: Sara Kidd

FOR READER'S DIGEST
U.S. Project Editor: Jane Townswick
Canadian Project Editor: Pamela Johnson
Project Designer: Jennifer R. Tokarski
Executive Editor, Trade Publishing: Dolores York
Director, Trade Publishing: Christopher T. Reggio
Vice President & Publisher, Trade Publishing: Harold Clarke

Library of Congress Cataloging-in-Publication Data
Nicol, Gloria.
  Quick & Easy Home Sewing Projects: 50 low- and no-sew projects to enhance every room in your
home/ Gloria Nicol.
  p. cm.
ISBN 0-7621-0585-2
1. House furnishings. 2. Machine sewing. I. Title: Quick and easy home sewing projects. II. Title
TT387. N53 2005
646.2'1—dc22

2004051307

Printed in China

Address any comments about
Quick and Easy Home Sewing Projects to:
The Reader's Digest Association, Inc.
Adult Trade Publishing
Reader's Digest Road
Pleasantville, NY 10570-7000

Special thanks to Calico Corners, 681 East Main Street, Mt. Kisco, New York, for their generous
donation of fabrics.

For more Reader's Digest products and information, visit our website:
www.rd.com (in the United States)
www.rd.ca (in Canada)

10 9 8 7 6 5 4 3 2 1 (paperback)

Contents

chapter one

WINDOW TREATMENTS

An elegant approach to windows transforms a room.
In this chapter you will find simple-to-make swags,
pelmets, shades, and curtains that will create a
new look for the rooms in your home.

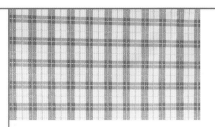

Curtain pole swag

A curtain pole swag tops a window in the same way as a pelmet or cornice and can be used with or without curtains underneath. This simply draped version has a softer, more casual style than formal swags and cascades, but the effect is similar. It can be used alone as a summer window treatment where curtains are dispensed with altogether and would also look good framing a doorway. Here, a simple plaid throw is lined with a solid-colored contrasting fabric, which can be glimpsed at the sides where the fabric falls in gentle folds. Cream fringing makes a luxurious edging that accentuates the shape of the folds.

You Will Need

- 3¼ yd. (3 m) of 54-in. (137-cm)-wide home decorating cotton
- 3¼ yd. (3 m) of 54-in. (137-cm)-wide coordinating fabric for the lining
- 2¼ yd. (2 m) of fringing
- matching sewing thread

Note: The swag measures 37 in. (93 cm) wide and 115 in. (290 cm) long, and would suit a 4–5-ft. (1.2–1.5-m) curtain pole. Adjust it to fit your own window.

Cutting Out

Note: Seam allowances of ⅝ in. (1.5 cm) are included throughout unless otherwise stated.

Cut a 37 x 116¼-in. (93 x 293-cm) rectangle from the main fabric for the top and a 39¼ x 116¼-in. (99 x 293-cm) rectangle from the coordinating fabric for the lining.

✓ 3 HOURS OR LESS

LOW-SEW PROJECT

The plaid pattern of the throw suits the rustic, country-style setting.

1 With right sides together, pin the top and lining rectangles together along a long edge and stitch. Press the seam open.

2 With right sides together, bring the long edges of both fabrics together and pin so a narrow border forms along the joined edge, which will be the front edge of the swag. Lay the fabrics down flat, measure 11 in. (28 cm) in from each short edge along the front edge, and mark with pins. Draw a line from each marked point to meet the back corners and cut away triangles of both fabrics following the lines.

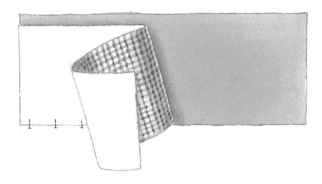

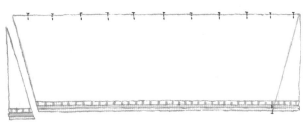

3 Pin the sloping edges together and stitch along both of them and the back edge, leaving an opening of approximately 12 in. (30 cm). Turn to the right side, turn under the edges of the opening, and slip stitch to close. Press along all edges.

4 Pin a length of fringing along the right side of each sloping edge, folding under a tiny amount at either end, and topstitch in place to secure.

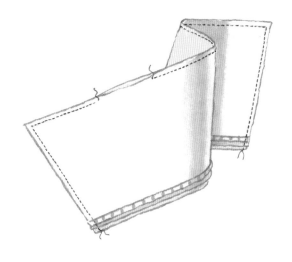

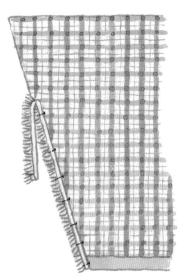

Toile de Jouy pelmet

Pelmets or cornices are the crowning glory when it comes to window dressing, and help to hide the mechanism of the curtain treatment underneath. Backing the pelmet with self-adhesive buckram makes it substantial and keeps it flat when mounted on a simple wood frame. Here, the pelmet is fitted to the outside of the window frame, so it needs only a shallow frame to allow it to stand away from the window. A classic toile de Jouy print is a light and pretty style suitable for a bathroom or bedroom. The dusty pink in the design has been picked out in a plain damask fabric, which is used to make a border that accentuates the sweeping curves of the pelmet edge.

You Will Need

- pattern paper and pencil
- 1 yd. (90 cm) fine piping cord and a 12 x 8-in. (30 x 20-cm) piece of the main fabric to make bias binding (optional)
- high-tack fabric adhesive
- ½ yd. (0.5 m) of 55-in. (140-cm)-wide home decorating cotton
- 5 in. (13 cm) of 54-in. (137-cm)-wide coordinating fabric
- 30-in. (80-cm) length of 18-in. (45-cm)-wide self-adhesive pelmet buckram
- packet of 8-in. (20-cm)-wide fusible web
- 4¾ ft. (145 cm) of ¾-in. (2-cm) wooden battens
- hand or electric drill
- six 2-in. (5-cm) screws
- small tacks and a hammer
- hacksaw
- matching sewing thread

Note: The pelmet measures 27½ x 14¾ in. (69 x 37 cm). Adjust to fit the size of your own window.

 3 HOURS OR LESS

 LOW-SEW PROJECT

This style of treatment is suited to traditional fabrics and a setting of formal elegance.

1 Make up the piping from some of the leftover main fabric (see page 155). Using fabric adhesive, glue it along the bottom edge of the pelmet so that the cord follows the shaped pelmet edge and the raw edges are to the inside. Cut notches in the bias binding seam allowance so that you can ease it around the curves. Place the shaped border along the bottom edge of the pelmet so that the piping shows below it and iron it in place. Topstitch along both sides of the border if you wish.

2 Cut a 27½-in. (69-cm) length of batten for the top of the frame and two 13¼-in. (34-cm) lengths for the sides. Drill two evenly spaced holes through each batten and screw them onto the window frame so that the corners make 90° angles.

3 Fold the top ¾ in. (2 cm) of the pelmet over the top of the frame and glue it in place, securing with a tack in the center and at each end. Trim the top corners, then fold the pelmet sides over the frame sides and glue them in place.

Cutting Out

Fold a 29 x 6-in. (73 x 15-cm) strip of paper in half widthwise. Measure 3¼ in. (8 cm) up from one long edge, and draw a line across the paper parallel to the edge. Starting 3¼ in. (8 cm) in from the bottom outside corner, draw a sweeping curve up to meet the line; draw another curve down to the bottom edge, and back up to the line at the center fold. Cut out the curve, cutting through both thicknesses of paper, and open out the paper to make a symmetrical shape.

Cut a 29 x 15½-in. (73 x 39-cm) rectangle from the main fabric. Following the manufacturer's instructions, stick self-adhesive buckram to the back of the fabric. Pin the paper template on the fabric, with the shaped edge of the template along the bottom edge of the fabric. Draw the curves on the fabric and cut it out.

On the paper template draw a border 1½ in. (3.5 cm) deep that follows the curves of the shaped edge and that comes up to a point in the center. Following the manufacturer's instructions, iron fusible web to the back of the coordinating fabric. Using the template, cut out one border piece.

Roller shade

This attractive roller shade has a shaped bottom edge, which echoes the edge of the pelmet above. The edges have also been faced with a pink damask fabric to coordinate with the pelmet. Roller shades require very little fabric, making them a very economical window dressing. All you need is a piece of fabric just big enough to cover the window, plus a little extra on the length to make a channel for the slat. Stiffen the fabric with a stiffening spray or by dipping it in a stiffening solution so that the edges will not fray, and make sure you cut the fabric perfectly square so that the shade will roll up evenly. Roller-shade kits are usually sized in 12-in. (30-cm) increments, so buy the kit that is the next size up from your window and cut the dowel roller to fit.

You Will Need

- pattern paper and pencil
- 1⅞ yd. (1.7 m) of 55-in. (140-cm)-wide home decorating cotton
- ¼ yd. (0.2 m) of 54-in. (137-cm)-wide coordinating fabric
- fabric stiffening spray or solution
- roller shade kit
- packet of 8-in. (20-cm)-wide fusible web
- 1 yd. (90 cm) fine piping cord (optional)
- fabric adhesive
- hacksaw
- matching sewing thread

Note: The shade measures 22 x 55 in. (56 x 140 cm). Adjust to fit your own window.

 3 HOURS OR LESS

 LOW-SEW PROJECT

A roller shade is ideal for narrow windows where curtains would look too bulky.

1 With right sides together, lay the side borders down the side edges of the shade and cut them along the bottom edges following the curve. Back the strips with fusible web and, following the manufacturer's instructions, iron them in place on the side edges of the shade. With some of the leftover main fabric, make up the piping, if using (see page 155).

2 Using fabric adhesive, glue the piping along the bottom edge of the shade, with the cord following the shaped edge and the raw edges to the inside. Back the shaped bottom-edge border with fusible web and iron it onto the bottom of the shade, so that the piping shows evenly below it. Topstitch along both sides of the border (optional).

3 Mark both side edges with pins 5½ in. (14 cm) up from the bottom corners. With right sides together, fold the fabric across the shade from pin to pin and machine stitch across the fabric 2 in. (5 cm) from the fold to make a channel across the back of the shade. Press the channel toward the bottom edge and work a line of open machine zigzag stitching across the shade over the seam.

4 Following the instructions supplied with the roller-shade kit, fix the top of the shade to the roller. Cut the slat 1½ in. (3.5 cm) narrower than the shade and push it through the channel. Slip stitch both ends of the channel closed. Thread the cord through the cord holder and screw it through the fabric to the center point of the slat. Fix the acorn to the other end, if using. Mount the brackets on the wall or window frame, and fit the roller in position.

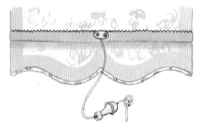

Cutting Out

Stiffen both the main and coordinating fabrics with fabric stiffening spray or soak in a stiffening solution. Leave the fabrics to dry before you cut them to size.

From the main fabric, cut a 22 x 65-in. (56 x 165-cm) rectangle, following the grain. Following the instructions for the toile de Jouy pelmet on page 9, make a paper template 4½ in. (11 cm) deep for the shaped bottom edge. Cut away the same amount from

each side, so that the template is the same width as the shade. Place the paper template on the bottom edge of the main fabric, draw around it, and cut it out.

On the template draw a border 1½ in. (3.5 cm) deep that follows the curves of the shaped edge with a point in the center. Using the template, cut a border piece from the coordinating fabric and two side borders 1½ in. (3.5 cm) wide and 55 in. (140 cm) long.

Triple-pleated drapery heading with buttons

Drapery headings set the style for window treatments—formal or informal, soft and casual, or neat and tidy. Triple-pleated headings create a grand style suitable for big windows and long drapes. The pleats can be made by hand; alternatively, you can buy a special heading tape that automatically gathers into a triple-pleat formation—although you still need to work out where the pleats will form in order to calculate the finished width of the shade. A button to cover on each pleat emphasizes the heading. Choose a coordinating fabric for the lining so that the drape will look just as good from either side.

You Will Need

- 5 yd. (4.5 m) of 55-in. (140-cm)-wide home decorating cotton plus the depth of one pattern repeat
- 4¾ yd. (4.3 m) of 55-in. (140-cm)-wide curtain lining
- 2¾ yd. (2.5 m) of triple-pleat heading tape
- nine 1¼-in. (28-mm) buttons to cover
- curtain hooks
- matching sewing thread

Note: The drapery measures 42 x 81 in. (106 x 205 cm) when the heading is pleated. Adjust to fit your own window.

Cutting Out

Note: Seam allowances of ⅝ in. (1.5 cm) are included throughout unless otherwise stated.

Calculate the positions of the pleats before you cut the fabric. From the main fabric, cut two matching lengths 48 in. (122 cm) wide x 89 in. (225 cm) long, taking the pattern repeat into consideration. From the lining fabric, cut two lengths 46¾ in. (119 cm) wide x 83½ in. (212 cm) long.

6 TO 8 HOURS

SEW PROJECT

1 With right sides together, pin the two main fabric pieces together along the center front edge, matching the pattern across the seam, and machine stitch. Press the seam open. Join the two lining pieces in the same way.

Floor-length drapes are an economical and stylish form of draft insulation.

2 Turn under ⅜ in. (1 cm) then 1⅝ in. (4 cm) along the bottom edge of the lining, pin, and machine stitch. With right sides together, pin the lining to the main fabric along one side edge, mark with a pin 10½ in. (27 cm) up from the bottom edge of the main piece, and stitch between the top edge and the pin marker. Join the other side of the lining to the other side of the main fabric piece in the same way. Press the seams toward the lining.

3 Turn the curtain right side out. With wrong sides together, press the side edges so that the lining is centered on the back with an even border of the main fabric on each side. Pin, then baste the lining and main fabrics together along the top edge. Turn under 2 in. (5 cm) along the top edge.

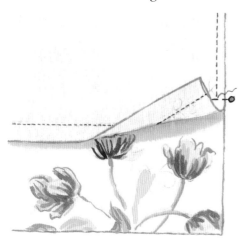

4 Turn under 1 in. (3 cm), then 5 in. (12 cm) along the bottom edge of the main piece and baste, folding in the corners to meet the lining hem. Hand stitch the hem in place, mitering the corners (see pages 149–150).

5 Slip stitch the bottom side edges of the lining to the borders at each side and slip stitch along the bottom edges of the lining for 1¼ in. (3 cm).

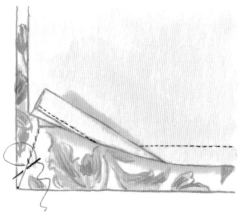

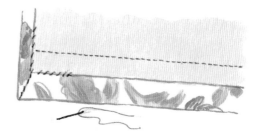

6 Pin the heading tape to the wrong side ¼ in. (6 mm) down from the top, placing the pleats so there will be an equal flat area at each end. Turn under ½ in. (12 mm) at each end of the tape, leaving the cords free at one end. Stitch in place along all four edges of the tape.

7 Pull the free ends of the cords to gather the heading into triple pleats to the required width, arranging the pleats neatly. Knot the cords to secure.

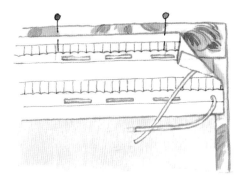

8 Cover the buttons following the manufacturer's instructions. On the right side of the curtain, make a few stitches by hand along the bottom edge of each pleat, stitching through all the layers to hold the pleat in place. Hand stitch a button over the stitching on each pleat.

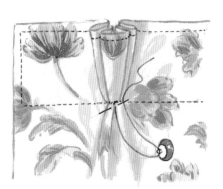

Professional's Tip: Pleating

Triple pleats (also called pinch pleats) are the most popular heading style for floor-length draperies, and there are several ways of making them.

■ As an alternative to the corded style of pleat tape shown, you could use the type made with pockets, into which you insert special hooks with four prongs, which automatically form a triple pleat. Before cutting out the fabric, insert the hooks into the tape pockets at the chosen intervals. This will establish the pleated width of the drapery panel.

■ Trim the tape, leaving an allowance for turning under, and remove the hooks. Cut the fabric so that the width equals the length of the tape when flat, plus an allowance for side hems.

Tieback

Tiebacks hold your drapes neatly out of the way when they aren't needed and become a decorative feature in their own right. They can be made in a matching or a contrasting fabric. To work out how long the tieback needs to be, pass a tape measure around the shade, holding the folds of fabric to approximate how you want it to look. The tieback should normally be positioned about two-thirds of the way down from the top. Hooks fixed to the wall or window frame are needed to hold the tieback securely in place. Here, the tieback is made in the same fabric as the drape, with a contrasting bound edge to finish it off. An iron-on buckram interlining fuses the fabric and lining together and means that very little sewing is required.

You Will Need

- 28 x 6 in. (71 x 15 cm) piece of home decorating cotton
- 28 x 6 in. (71 x 15 cm) piece of contrasting fabric
- 20-in. (51-cm) strip of 6-in. (15-cm)-wide fusible buckram
- 2 rings
- matching sewing thread

Note: The tieback measures 5½ x 27½ in. (14 x 70 cm). Adjust it to fit your own window.

Cutting Out

Note: Seam allowances of ⅝ in. (1.5 cm) are included throughout unless otherwise stated.

Using the pattern, cut out one piece each from the main fabric, lining, and buckram. Cut out 1½-in.- (36-mm)-wide bias strips and join them together (see page 154) to make a 63-in. (160-cm) length.

3 HOURS OR LESS

LOW-SEW PROJECT

A contrasting edge helps to define the shape of the tieback.

1 Place the main fabric and lining pieces wrong sides together, with the buckram sandwiched in between. Followingthe fusible buckram manufacturer's instructions, press the fabrics with a hot iron to fuse the layers together.

2 With the right side of the binding to the front of the tieback, pin the binding around the edge, joining the ends where they meet (see page 155). Machine stitch, using a ½-in. (12-mm) seam, trim the seam to ¼ in. (6 mm), and turn the binding to the back of the tieback.

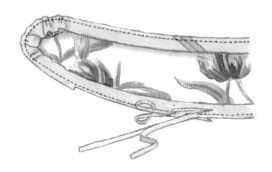

3 Turn under the edge of the binding by ⅜ in. (9 mm)and slip stitch it in place all around (see page 149) with matching sewing thread to the back of the tieback.

4 Hand stitch a ring to each end of the tieback on the underside of the curve, working a few slip stitches through each ring.

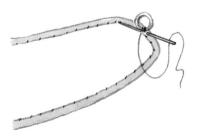

Professional's Tip: Making the Pattern

Make a pattern by folding a 28 x 6-in. (71 x 15-cm) piece of paper in half widthwise so that the folded edge will be the center of the tieback. On the bottom edge, mark a point 3 in. (7.5 cm) from the fold. Draw a gentle curve up to meet the opposite edge approximately 2½ in. (6 cm) down from the corner. Curve around to meet the top edge about 3 in. (7.5 cm) from the corner, then sweep down to a point 1¼ in. (3 cm) from the top, on the fold. Cut out the paper shape, then open it out so you can see the whole shape, and adjust the curves if necessary.

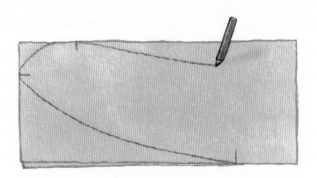

Ribbon tied-top curtain

A delicate translucent fabric such as voile or georgette makes a romantic treatment for French doors or long windows—the curtain will billow in the slightest breeze. This sumptuous embroidered georgette fabric is edged top and bottom with borders made from linen, with satin ribbon decorating the seams. The same ribbon is used to make simple ties along the top of the curtain. Here the full width of the fabric is used to make a complete panel, which looks good just gently gathered. For a wider window, make two matching panels rather than joining them.

You Will Need

- 1⅞ yd. (1.7 m) of 60-in. (150-cm)-wide embroidered georgette or voile
- ⅞ yd. (0.8 cm) of 60-in. (150-cm)-wide cotton or linen
- 9½ yd. (8.7 m) of ½-in. (12-mm)-wide ribbon
- matching sewing thread

Note: The curtain measures 56 in. (142 cm) wide and 80 in. (203 cm) long. Adjust it to fit your own window.

Cutting Out

Note: Seam allowances of ⅝ in. (1.5 cm) are included throughout unless otherwise stated.

Cut a 63¼ x 60-in. (161 x 150-cm) rectangle of georgette or voile. Cut two 7¼ x 60-in. (18.5 x 150-cm) linen strips for the top border and a 14 x 60-in. (34.5 x 150-cm) linen rectangle for the bottom border.

⏱ 3 HOURS OR LESS

🖶 SEW PROJECT

Lightweight curtains are perfect for letting in a gentle breeze in the summer months.

1 With wrong sides together, pin the bottom border to the bottom edge of the georgette or voile and machine stitch. Trim the seam and press toward the border. Pin a length of ribbon over the seam to cover the raw edges and topstitch in place, stitching close to both edges.

2 Cut off the selvages from both side edges. Turn under ⅜ in. (1 cm), then ½ in. (12 mm) down each side edge and machine stitch. Turn under ½ in. (12 mm), then ¾ in. (2 cm) along the bottom border edge and machine stitch.

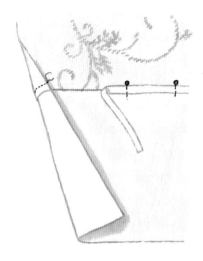

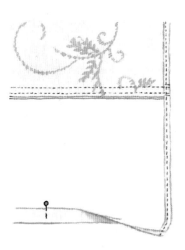

3 Cut ten 22-in. (56-cm) lengths of ribbon, and fold each in half widthwise. Pin the ribbons to the right side of the top edge of one top border piece, with the folds along the raw edge, positioning one ribbon 1 in. (2.5 cm) in from each end and spacing the remaining eight pieces evenly in between. With right sides together, pin the two top border strips together along the top edge, so that the ribbons are sandwiched between, and machine stitch. Turn right side out and press.

4 With right sides together, pin the lower edge of the top border front piece to the top edge of the panel; machine stitch. Turn right side out and press the seam. With right sides of the border pieces together, pin then stitch down the short side edges so the seam is in line with the hemmed side edges of the panel. Trim the seams, turn the top border to the right side, and press. Turn under ⅝ in. (1.5 cm) along the lower edge of the top border back piece, press, pin to the panel along the seam line, and stitch. On the front, pin ribbon over the seam, turning under the ends, and topstitch in place, stitching close to both edges of the ribbon.

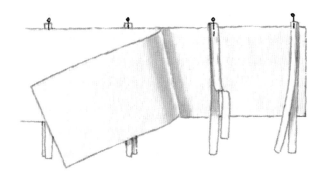

Braid-trimmed curtains

Long drapes made entirely from the same solid or small-patterned weaves can look monotonous, but sewing bands of cotton tape or ribbon horizontally across the fabric is a simple way of changing the proportions and breaking up large areas. Use tape or ribbon in varying widths and position them so that they align when the curtains are closed. To work out the position of the bands, lay the curtains flat on the floor and experiment with different placements. Only one width of fabric was needed for each of the curtains shown here. For a bigger window, join widths of fabric to make the curtains wider (see page 157).

(see page 157)

 6 TO 8 HOURS

SEW PROJECT

1 Cut the selvages off the sides of the main fabric pieces. Pin the cotton tape to the right side of the fabric across both main pieces so that they align, placing the wide tape 13½ in. (34 cm) up from the bottom edge and the narrow tape 1¼ in. (3 cm) above it. Topstitch in place, stitching close to both edges of the tapes.

The bands of tape used here help to balance the curtains against the windowsill.

21

2 Turn under ⅜ in. (1 cm), then 1½ in. (4 cm) along the bottom edge of the lining, pin, and machine stitch. With right sides together, pin the lining to the main fabric along one side edge. Place a pin 10½ in. (27 cm) up from the bottom edge of the main piece, and stitch between the top edge and the pin marker. Join the other side edge of the lining to the other side edge of the main piece in the same way. Press the seams toward the lining.

3 Turn to the right side and press the side edges so that the lining is centered on the back, with an equal border of the main fabric on each side. Pin, then baste the lining and main fabrics together along the top edge.

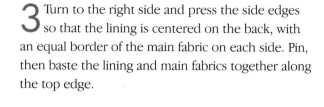

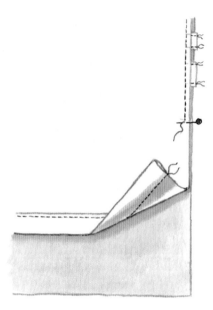

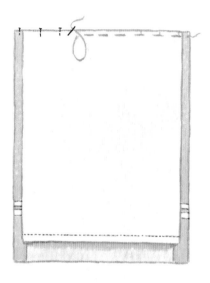

4 Turn under ⅝ in. (1.5 cm), then 4¾ in. (12 cm) along the bottom edge of the main piece and baste, folding in the corners to meet the lining hem and mitering the corners (see page 150). Hand stitch the hem in place (see page 149).

5 Slip stitch the bottom side edges of the lining to the borders at each side and slip stitch along the bottom edges of the lining for 1¼ in. (3 cm).

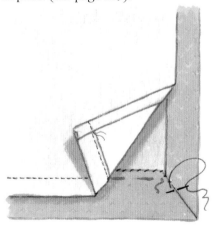

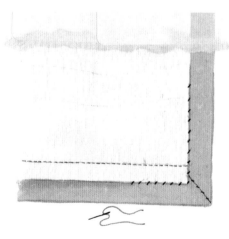

6 Turn under 2 in. (5 cm) along the curtain top edge. Pin the heading tape to the wrong side, ¼ in. (6 mm) down from the top. Turn under ½ in. (12 mm) at each end. Stitch in place along all four edges of the tape.

7 Pull the free ends of the cords to gather the heading to the required width. Knot the cords to secure. Make up the other curtain in the same way, pulling the cords at the other end of the tape on that curtain.

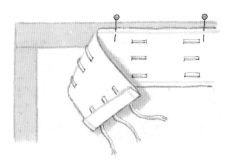

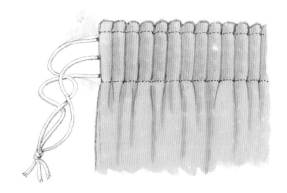

Professional's Tip: Training Curtains

Floor-length curtains should hang in straight, graceful folds. This is especially important in a style such as this one, with its simple horizontal trimming. For a professional look, "train" them after hanging.

■ First cut eight or ten lengths of ribbon or woven tape, long enough to tie around each panel when the curtains are fully open.
■ With the curtains opened, use both hands to smooth the fabric into even folds. Keep the folds stacked together as you go, and make sure that both edges point toward the wall/window. Tie a ribbon around the curtain panel to hold the pleats in place (but not so tightly as to crease the fabric). Tie other ribbons, evenly spaced, above and below the first.
■ Leave the ribbons in place for about four or five days to allow the pleats to set.
■ To attach the curtains to the rod, fit curtain hooks into the pockets in the heading, and insert the hooks into the sliders on the rod.

Gathered shade

This simple shade is flat and unobtrusive when down and has an easy casual style when pulled up. Just two cords raise the blind to the required height, and lengths of ribbon, in matching or contrasting colors, can be used to make decorative ties around the shade but are an optional extra. Screw eyes along the top are fixed to L-shaped hooks on the window frame, making the shade extremely simple to fit and easy to remove. The style is informal and would suit a bedroom, beach-house, or summerhouse. The cream and primrose-yellow striped linen used here has a clean fresh look that is ideal for the summer months. Striped and checked fabrics are especially suitable.

1 With right sides together, pin one long edge of the lining piece to one short edge of the main piece and machine stitch. Pin the other long edge of the lining piece to the other short edge of the main piece and stitch in the same way. Press the seam open.

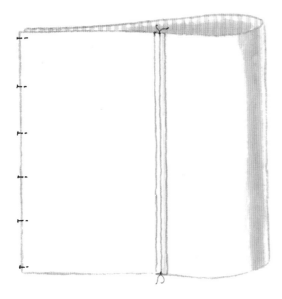

This simple shade has clean lines and an understated style that would suit most windows.

You Will Need

- 1½ yd. (1.4 m) of 55-in. (140 cm)-wide home decorating fabric
- ⅞ yd. (0.8 m) of 55-in. (140-cm)-wide curtain lining
- 40-in. (102-cm)-long 1⅜ x ⅝-in. (3.5 x 1.5-cm) wooden batten
- twenty ½-in. (12-mm) plastic rings and five screw eyes
- bradawl
- 4 yd. (3.7 m) nylon cord
- acorn and awning cleat
- two L-shaped hooks
- matching sewing thread
- 3½ yd. (3.2 m) of 1¼-in. (3-cm)-wide grosgrain ribbon (optional)

Note: The shade measures 41½ in. (105 cm) wide x 47¾ in. (121 cm) long. Adjust it to fit your own window.

Cutting Out

Note: Seam allowances of ⅝ in. (1.5 cm) are included throughout unless otherwise stated.

Cut a 54¾ x 53½-in. (138 x 135.5-cm) rectangle from the main fabric for the front and a 30¾ x 53½-in. (78 x 135.5-cm) rectangle from the lining fabric.

6 TO 8 HOURS

SEW PROJECT

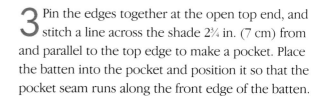

2 With right sides together, fold the side edges so that the lining is centered on the back of the shade and pin along one open end, which will be the bottom edge of the shade. Stitch, then turn to the right side, and press flat so that the side edges are straight.

3 Pin the edges together at the open top end, and stitch a line across the shade 2¾ in. (7 cm) from and parallel to the top edge to make a pocket. Place the batten into the pocket and position it so that the pocket seam runs along the front edge of the batten.

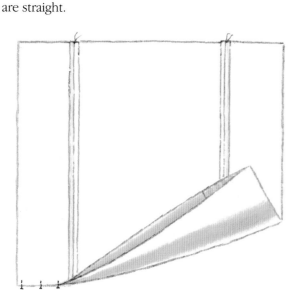

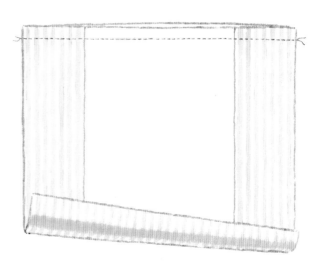

4 Fold the back of the shade around the batten and fold the front of the pocket around in the other direction to completely encase it. Fold in the edges and slip stitch the fabric securely in place.

5 On the back of the shade, mark the position of the rings along both seamlines where the main fabric and the lining meet, the first ones 1¼ in. (3 cm) up from the bottom edge and the rest spaced at 4¾-in. (12-cm) intervals. Hand stitch a ring in position at each mark, stitching through each ring a few times.

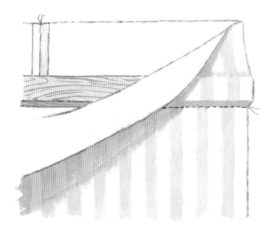

6 Turn the covered batten over to the inside so that the shade runs flat down the front. Using a bradawl, make a small hole through the fabric and into the wood at each side where the lining and main fabric meet, in line with the rings. Make another hole in the underside of the batten ¾ in. (2 cm) in from the end from which the cords will operate, and screw in another screw eye. Make two holes and insert screw eyes in the top, in line with the rings.

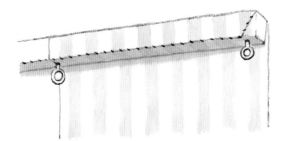

7 Tie a length of cord to each bottom ring and thread up through the rings and the screw eyes on the underside of the batten, toward the side from which they will be pulled to raise or lower the shade. Thread the ends together through an acorn, and knot to secure.

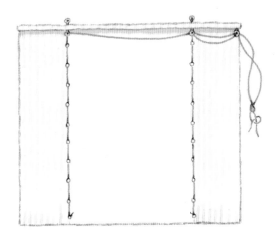

8 Mount the shade on the window frame with two L-shaped hooks spaced to match the screw eyes along the top of the batten. If you wish, cut the ribbon into two equal lengths and tie around the shade in line with the rings. Affix an awning cleat to the side of the window frame.

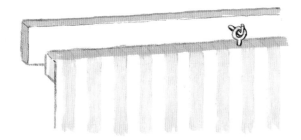

Professional's Tip: Ribbon Ties

Lengths of grosgrain ribbon tied under the shade make a perfect finishing touch.

■ The amount of ribbon specified on page 25 can be knotted about 25 in. (64 cm) from the top, leaving ties about 5–6 in. (13–15 cm) long. For longer or shorter ties, allow twice the length at which the shade will normally hang, plus at least 12 in. (30 cm). For additional flexibility, add a little more; when the shades are pulled higher, the ribbon can then be tied in a bow, instead of a knot.

■ The midpoint of the ribbon can be attached to the batten with tacks or with fabric glue. For easy removal when washing or dry-cleaning the shade, attach the ribbon to the fabric with a few stitches.

Roman shade

A slatted Roman shade forms neat soft folds when raised and has a simple, unfussy style when lowered. Slats sewn into the structure of the shade give it weight, so the folds form neatly. A heavy brass acorn is another useful device, providing enough weight to keep the cords taut. If the shade is wider than your fabric, join widths to form a wide central panel with a narrower panel on either side and match the fabric pattern across the seams. Here, a pompom trimming has been used along the bottom edge and cotton tape sewn down each side to make a striking decorative detail.

1 With right sides together, pin the facing to one short edge of the lining. Machine stitch, then press the seam open. Press under the seam allowance along the other short edge of the lining, which will be the top edge of the shade. Pin a length of tape to the right side of the front, parallel to and 6 in. (15 cm) in from each side edge, and topstitch in place, stitching down both edges of the tape.

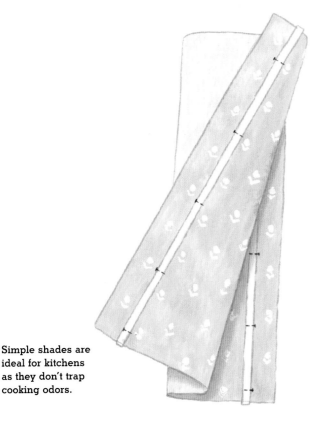

Simple shades are ideal for kitchens as they don't trap cooking odors.

You Will Need

- 2 yd. (1.7 m) of 54-in. (137-cm)-wide home decorating cotton
- 1½ yd. (1.3 m) of 54-in. (137-cm)-wide curtain lining
- 3½ yd. (3 m) of 1-in. (2.5-cm)-wide cotton tape
- 1½ yd. (1.2 m) of pompom braid
- masking tape
- 1½ yd. (1.2 m) of 2-in. (5-cm)-wide Velcro tape
- five 45½ x ⅞ x ¼-in. (116 x 22 x 7-mm) wooden battens
- twenty ⅝-in. (15-mm) plastic rings
- four ⅝-in. (15-mm) screw eyes
- 44½-in. (113-cm) length of 2 x 1¼-in. (5 x 3-cm) wooden batten
- staple gun or small tacks
- 12 yd. (11 m) of nylon cord
- matching sewing thread
- shade acorn and awning cleat

Note: The shade measures 46 x 57 in. (117 x 145 cm). Adjust it to fit your own window.

Cutting Out

Note: Seam allowances of ⅝ in. (1.5 cm) are included throughout unless otherwise stated.

From the main fabric, cut a 47¼ x 58¼-in. (120 x 148-cm) rectangle for the front and a 47¼ x 7¼-in. (120 x 18-cm) strip for the facing. From the lining fabric, cut a 47¼ x 52¼-in. (120 x 133-cm) rectangle.

6 TO 8 HOURS

SEW PROJECT

2 Press under the seam allowance along the top edge of the front. Pin the pompom braid to the bottom edge of the front on the right side, so that the pompoms face inward and lie just inside the seam allowance; baste in place by hand. With right sides together, pin the front and lining pieces together so that the facing on the lining piece is next to the pompom edge. Along each side edge, place one pin level with the seam that joins the facing to the lining, with a second pin 1¼ in. (3 cm) above it, to mark the position for the first batten pocket. Mark the other four pocket positions in the same way, leaving a 10-in. (25-cm) gap between the pockets. Machine stitch down both sides and along the bottom edge, leaving the top edge, and the gaps between the pin markers for the pockets, open.

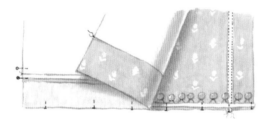

3 Turn the shade right side out and press along the edges. Apply strips of masking tape across the fabric from side to side to mark the edges of the batten pockets. Following the tape guides, stitch through all layers to make the pockets. Pin the sew-on side of the Velcro along the wrong side of the top edge and machine stitch it in place.

4 Cut the battens slightly shorter than the width of the shade. Thread them through the pockets and slip stitch the ends closed.

5 Mark the positions of the rings on the back along the top edge of each batten by inserting one pin 2 in. (5 cm) in from each side edge, with two more pins evenly spaced in between. Hand stitch a ring in place at each pin marker.

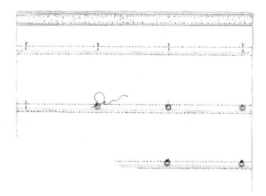

6 Screw four screw eyes, spaced in the same way as the rings, into the bottom edge of the wood batten fixed above the window. Stick the other side of the Velcro to the front of the batten and also secure it with evenly spaced staples or tacks. Hang up the shade by pushing the Velcro strips together.

7 Working from the back of the shade, thread four varying lengths of cord one by one through the screw eyes and down through the rings, securing the cord each time by knotting it to the bottom ring. Where the four cords meet at the top of the shade, thread them through the acorn and knot them together, adjusting the length to suit the window. Fix an awning cleat to the side of the window frame.

Professional's Tip: Trimmings

The pompom braid used to trim this shade will suit modern or traditional decor, provided it is fairly informal. For a more formal or romantic style of room, simply choose a trimming to enhance that effect.

■ Elegant ready-made trimmings, such as fringes, are available in home decorating stores and departments and via the Internet.

■ For a more adventurous, modern look, choose subtle trimmings such as a traditional braid with a glitter thread running through it, ideal for enhancing light at the window.

■ If you can crochet, you could make your own trimming, using crochet cotton to match or contrast with your fabric. Begin by working one or two repeats of the pattern. Pin the sample to an ironing board, and block or press it into shape. Use this sample to calculate how long a piece you will need to fit the lower edge of the shade.

■ Attach the edging to the shade by hand, with tiny slip stitches.

Balloon shade

These shades do sometimes need dressing when they are pulled up, so are ideal for rooms where they can be left raised most of the time. Alternatively, they can be used as part of a window treatment with working curtains or a roller shade underneath. The pencil-pleat heading requires two to two-and-a-half widths of fabric.

You Will Need

- 3⅞ yd. (3.6 m) of 55-in. (140-cm)-wide home decorating fabric, plus the depth of one pattern repeat for matching the pattern (see page 157)
- 2¾ yd. (2.6 m) of 55-in. (140-cm)-wide curtain lining
- 2¾ yd. (2.5 m) of ready-made piping or 2¾ yd. (2.5m) piping cord and a 12 x 20-in. (30 x 50-cm) piece of contrasting cotton fabric
- 6¼ yd. (5.7 m) of balloon shade tape
- 2¾ yd. (2.5m) of 3-in. (7.5-cm)-wide pencil-pleat heading tape
- 20 screw eyes
- bradawl
- 8½ yd. (7.8 m) of nylon shade cord
- 15 curtain hooks
- 38-in. (97-cm)-long 2 x 1¼-in. (5 x 3-cm) wooden batten fitted along the top of the window frame
- acorn and awning cleat
- matching sewing thread

Note: The shade fits a window approximately 40 in. (102 cm) wide and 42 in. (107 cm) long. It measures 93 in. (236 cm) wide and 56 in. (142 cm) long when flat (including the ruffle). Adjust it to fit your own window.

6 TO 8 HOURS

LOW-SEW PROJECT

This balloon shade has a generous ruched look that suits crisp fabrics.

1 With right sides together, pin, then stitch the two front pieces together, matching the pattern down the center. Press the seam open. Raw edges together, pin the piping along the bottom edge on the right side of the fabric, with the cord lying just inside the seamline, then baste by hand.

2 With right sides together, pin two ruffle pieces together along one short edge, stitch, and press the seam open. Join the other two strips in the same way, then join these two pieces to make one long strip. With right sides together, fold the ruffle strip in half lengthwise, pin together at the ends, and stitch.

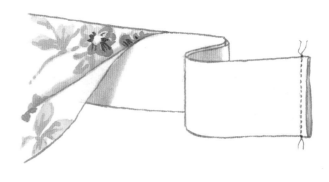

3 Trim the seams, turn to the right side, and press flat. With right sides out, baste the raw edges together by hand.

Cutting Out

Note: Seam allowances of ⅝ in. (1.5 cm) are included throughout unless otherwise stated.

From the main fabric, cut two 47¾ x 55-in. (121 x 140-cm) matching lengths for the front of the shade, taking the pattern repeat into consideration, and four 7¼ x 47¾-in. (18 x 121-cm) strips for the ruffle.

From the lining fabric, cut two 47¾ x 55-in. (121 x 140-cm) rectangles.

If you are making your own piping, cut bias strips from the contrasting fabric and make up 2¾ yd. (2.4 m) of piping (see page 155).

4 Gather the ruffle evenly along the raw edge with two rows of long machine stitch, pulling the bobbin threads so it fits across the bottom edge of the shade. With raw edges together and starting and ending ⅝ in. (1.5 cm) in from each end of the shade, pin the ruffle over the piping. Baste the ruffle in place by hand.

5 With right sides together, pin the lining to the shade and stitch down both side edges and along the bottom edge to secure the ruffle and piping. Turn to the right side and press the edges. Pin the lining and front edges together along the top edge. Fold over and press 1½ in. (4 cm) to the wrong side along the top edge and baste by hand.

6 Cut four matching lengths of balloon shade tape to fit the length of the shade from the ruffled edge to 3 in. (7.5 cm) from the top, making sure the cord channels will align across the shade. Pin both outside lengths of tape 1½ in. (4 cm) in from the side edges and machine stitch in place, stitching down both sides of the tape. Spacing them evenly, pin the remaining two lengths in between and machine stitch in place as before.

7 Pin the heading tape across the top of the shade ⅝ in. (1.5 cm) down from the folded top edge. Knot the cords at one end and leave them free at the other. Turn the ends of the tape under and stitch in place along all four edges of the tape.

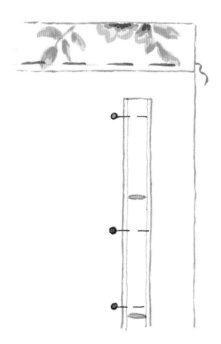

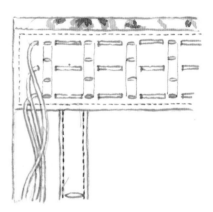

8 Using a bradawl, make four small holes along the bottom edge of the wooden batten and screw a screw eye into each one, with one screw eye 1¾ in. (4.5 cm) in from each end and the remaining two spaced evenly in between. Attach another screw eye along the same edge 1 in. (2.5 cm) in from the end from which the cords will be pulled. Make fifteen evenly spaced holes along the front edge of the batten, 1 in. (2.5 cm) down from the top edge, with the end holes 1¼ in. (3 cm) in from either end and the remaining thirteen spaced evenly. Screw a screw eye into each one. Gather up the heading tape by pulling the cords until the shade fits the window.

9 Knot the cords. Thread equally spaced curtain hooks through the top channel along the tape so that each one corresponds to a screw eye on the batten, then hook the shade in position at the window. Thread a length of cord up through each of the four channels running the length of the shade, through the screw eye above each channel, and through the eyes toward the side from which the cords will be pulled, fixing each cord to the first channel with a knot. Thread the hanging cords together through an acorn and knot to secure to create the pulley. Affix an awning cleat.

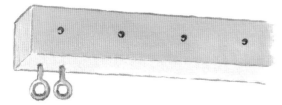

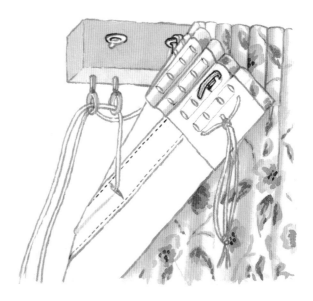

Professional's Tip: Gathering

When gathering a long piece of fabric, such as this ruffle, it's best to divide the work into segments.
■ Divide both edges into the same number of equal sections.
■ Work the gathering on the right side, so that the looser bobbin threads will be on top for pulling. Two rows of stitches, straddling the seamline, give smoother gathers.
■ Pin each section of ruffle to the straight piece, matching the divisions. Fasten the threads at one end around a pin. Pull on the other ends until the ruffle fits the edge; anchor the threads, then adjust the gathers, pinning the pieces together at short intervals. Baste.
■ Stitch the seam between the two gathering threads, which can then be removed.

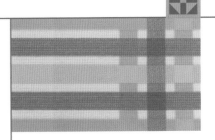

Gathered valance

A lined valance makes a soft, fluted edging for a country-style window treatment. Narrow shirring tape is used here: it needs to be sewn at least 1½ in. (4 cm) below the top of the valance in order to conceal the rod. Other kinds of heading tapes are also suitable for valance headings; refer to the fabric quantity guidelines on page 157 to see how many widths of fabric you need for the different types. This plaid fabric in fresh shades of green and blue would look just as good with matching curtains beneath but, here, has simple translucent voile curtains below, gathered on a separate curtain rod.

You Will Need

- ¾ yd. (60 cm) of 54-in. (137-cm)-wide home decorating fabric plus the depth of a pattern repeat
- ¾ yd. (60 cm) of 54-in. (137-cm)-wide lining fabric
- 2½-yd. (2.2 m) of shirring tape
- curtain hooks
- matching sewing thread

Note: The valance measures 10 x 86 in. (25.5 x 218 cm) to fit a curtain rod approximately 3–4 ft. (91–122 cm) long. Adjust it to fit your own window.

Cutting Out

Note: Seam allowances of ⅝ in. (1.5 cm) are included throughout unless otherwise stated.

From the main fabric, cut two 11¼ x 44¼-in. (28.5 x 112-cm) matching strips, taking any pattern repeat into consideration. From the lining fabric, cut two 11¼ x 44¼-in. (28.5 x 112-cm) strips.

3 HOURS OR LESS

LOW-SEW PROJECT

1 With right sides together, pin the two main fabric strips together along one short edge, matching the pattern, and machine stitch together. Press the seam open.

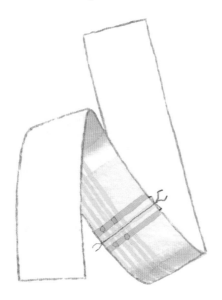

A gathered valance adds interest to an otherwise plain window treatment.

2 With right sides together, pin the two strips of lining together along one short edge and machine stitch. Press the seam open.

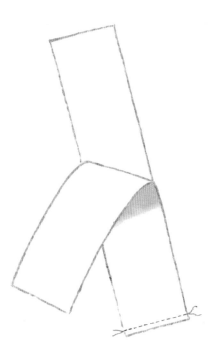

3 With right sides together, pin the main piece to the lining and machine stitch along all four sides, leaving a 10-in. (25-cm) opening along the top edge.

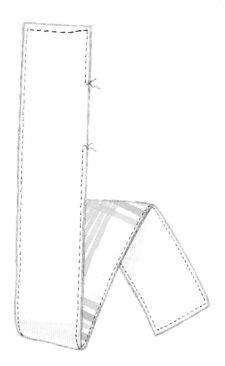

4 Trim the corners, turn the valance right side out, and press under the seam allowance along the edges of the opening. Slip stitch to close the opening and press.

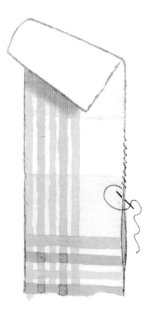

5 Pin the heading tape to the wrong side along the top, 1½ in. (4 cm) down from the top edge. Knot the cords at one end, and leave them free at the other. Turn under ½ in. (12 mm) of tape at each end. Machine stitch the tape in place, stitching close to all four edges.

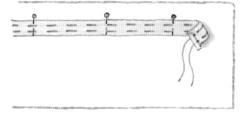

6 Pull the free ends of the cords, arranging the gathers evenly across the valance until it fits the rod. To affix the valance to the rod, fit curtain hooks into the pockets in the heading, and hook into the slides on the rod.

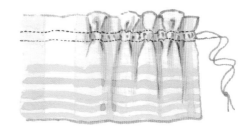

Professional's Tip: Making Gathers to the Correct Width

If you try to gather all the shirring tape in one go without working out your measurements in advance, the chances are that you'll pull the tape too tight and find that the final width of your gathered curtain or valance is too narrow for your window space.

First mark the quarter, halfway, and three-quarter points across the width of the fabric. Then measure the window space to work out how wide the valance or curtain needs to be when gathered, and divide

this measurement by four to find out how wide each quarter-section needs to be. Working from the center of the fabric to the first quarter-way point, pull the heading tape to gather the fabric to the required width. Tweak the gathers with your fingers to make sure they're evenly spaced: it's much easier to do this over a relatively narrow piece of fabric.

Repeat, working from the center point to the three-quarter-way point, and then again for the two outer sections of the fabric.

chapter two

BED LINENS

Surprisingly easy to make, fresh new bed linens offer an instant makeover for any bedroom. This section shows you how to create matching sets of linen as well as finishing touches such as bolsters and lavender pillows.

Ruffled pillowcase

A contrasting ruffle on a pillowcase creates a soft, romantic look, which you can echo by placing a matching dust ruffle over the base of the bed. Choose a floral or checked pattern for the main part of the pillowcase, then pick out a solid color from the design for the ruffle.

You Will Need

- 1¼ yd. (1.1 m) of 54-in. (137-cm)-wide cotton fabric
- 1¾ yd. (1.6 m) of 36-in. (90-cm)-wide cotton fabric for the ruffle
- matching sewing thread

Note: The pillowcase fits a standard pillow measuring 30 x 20 in. (75 x 50 cm).

Cutting Out

Note: Seam allowances of ⅝ in. (1.5 cm) are included throughout unless otherwise stated.

Cut two 31¼ x 21¼-in. (78 x 53-cm) pieces from the main fabric for the front and back and a 9½ x 21¼-in. (24 x 53-cm) piece for the flap. From the ruffle fabric, cut two 63 x 7¼-in. (159 x 19-cm) strips for the top and bottom ruffles and two 43½ x 7¼-in. (109 x 19-cm) strips for the side ruffles.

1 Turn under a ⅜-in. (1-cm) hem, followed by a ⅝-in. (1.5-cm) hem, along one short edge on the back piece, and machine stitch. Make a similar hem along one long edge of the flap piece.

⏱ 3 HOURS OR LESS

🪡 SEW PROJECT

Professional's Tip: Style Alternative

This design allows for great versatility if you need to create a set of pillowcases.
- For a double bed, reverse the use of plain and patterned fabric to make two cases with plain borders and two with patterned ones.
- For a single bed, use patterned fabric for the back of one pillowcase and front of the second pillowcase.

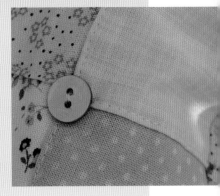

Plaid trims add style and an opportunity to introduce a range of colors into bed linen.

2 With right sides together, pin and then stitch a side-ruffle strip to a top-ruffle piece along one short edge. Press the seam open. Sew the other side ruffle to the other short end of the top-ruffle piece in the same way, and press the seam open. Sew the bottom ruffle to the remaining short edges of the side ruffles in the same way.

3 With wrong sides together, fold the assembled border in half lengthwise. Baste the raw edges together, and press. Gather the border into a ruffle along the raw (basted) edge, using a double length of thread if you're working by hand or the longest stitch setting on your machine if you're gathering by machine.

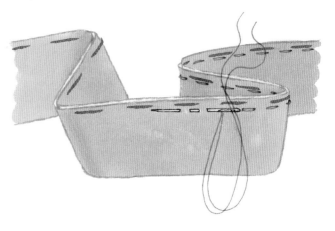

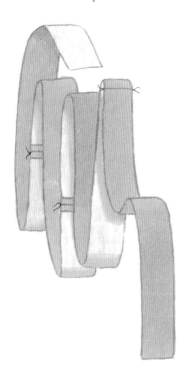

5 With right sides together, pin the back to the front with the ruffled border sandwiched between them and the unhemmed edge of the back piece aligning with one short raw edge of the front. Pin the flap right side down over the hemmed edge of the back piece, with the unhemmed edge of the flap aligning with the other short raw edge of the front piece, and machine stitch around all four sides. Zigzag the edges then turn the pillowcase right side out and press.

4 With raw edges together, pin the ruffle around the edge to the right side of the front gather, aligning the seams, and baste it in place.

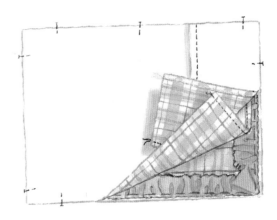

Border pillowcase with braid

Duck-egg blue and cream create a versatile color combination. The braid along the inside border edge is reminiscent of hand-stitched openwork embroidery.

1 Turn under a ⅜-in. (1-cm) hem followed by ⅝ in. (1.5 cm) along one short edge of the front piece and machine stitch. Repeat on one short edge of the back piece. Insert a pin 10½ in. (27 cm) from the hemmed edge on each long edge of the front to mark the fold line for the inside flap.

2 With right sides together, pin the front and back together, aligning the short raw edges. Fold the right side of the flap over to the wrong side of the back at the pin markers. Stitch around three sides, leaving the folded end open. Turn right side out and press. Pin braid all around the front so the inner edge is 2 in. (5 cm) in from the edges and topstitch.

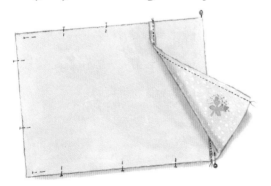

You Will Need

- 1½ yd. (1.2 m) of 54-in. (137-cm)-wide cotton fabric
- 3 yd. (2.7 m) of ⅜-in. (9-mm)-wide braid
- matching sewing thread

Note: The pillowcase fits a standard pillow measuring 30 x 20 in. (75 x 50 cm).

Cutting Out

Note: Seam allowances of ⅝ in. (1.5 cm) are included throughout, unless otherwise stated.

Cut a 46 x 25¼-in. (116 x 63-cm) rectangle for the front and a 33 x 25¼-in. (83 x 63-cm) rectangle for the back.

 3 HOURS OR LESS

 LOW-SEW PROJECT

Duvet cover with appliquéd center

A central panel in a floral fabric appliquéd to the front of the cover introduces a decorative element. To make bed linen in bigger sizes, piece the sections and stitch ribbon over the seams for a professional finish.

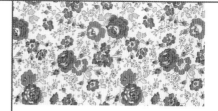

You Will Need

- 4¾ yd. (4.3 m) of 55-in. (140-cm)-wide cotton fabric
- 1¾ yd. (1.5 m) of 45-in. (115-cm)-wide coordinating cotton floral fabric
- 4⅞ yd. (4.5 m) of ¼-in. (6-mm)-wide ribbon
- six ⅝-in. (15-mm) buttons
- matching sewing thread

Note: The cover fits a standard duvet measuring 53½ x 80 in. (136 x 203 cm).

Cutting Out

Note: Seam allowances of ⅝ in. (1.5 cm) are included throughout unless otherwise stated.

Cut two 54¾ x 84-in. (139 x 213-cm) rectangles from the main fabric for the front and back. Cut out a 56¼ x 31¾-in. (143 x 81-cm) rectangle from the floral fabric for the front panel.

🕐 6 TO 8 HOURS

SEW PROJECT

A central panel in pretty contrasting fabric, such as that shown here, could be appliquéd to a plain ready-made duvet cover, too.

1 Turn under a hem of ⅜ in. (1 cm) then 1½ in. (4 cm) along a short edge of one of the main pieces to make the bottom edge of the front; stitch. Make a similar hem along the bottom edge of the other main piece for the back. Make six buttonholes along the hem of the back, placing the first and last ones 4 in. (10 cm) in from the sides and spacing the other four evenly in between.

2 Turn under the seam allowance on all four sides of the floral panel and press. With the wrong side of the panel to the right side of the cover front, pin the panel in the center of the front and topstitch in place close to the edges.

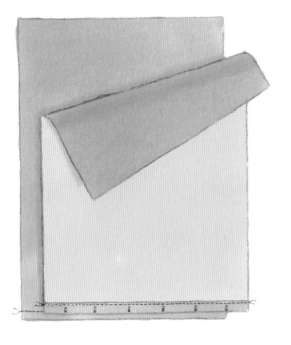

3 Pin the ribbon around the edges of the panel, making folds to turn the corners, then topstitch in place, stitching close to both edges of the ribbon. With right sides together, pin and stitch the front to the back along the side edges and top edge.

4 Neaten raw edges with a machine zigzag stitch, turn the cover right side out, and press. Turn the hemmed edge on both back and front to the inside of the cover and press. Topstitch close to both folds, stitching through all thicknesses of fabric for 2½ in. (6 cm) in from each side edge. Sew on buttons to correspond to each buttonhole.

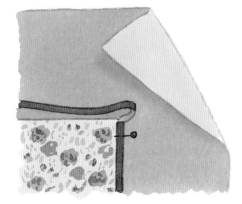

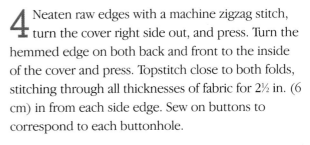

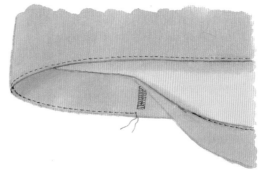

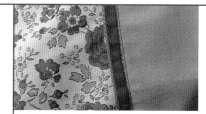

Matching pillowcase
This matching standard pillowcase is quick and simple to achieve. Symmetrical bands of coordinating floral fabric break up the solid-color fabric to make pretty deep-bordered edges. Lines of ribbon, topstitched in place, offer a further decorative detail as well as covering the raw edges.

You Will Need

- 1¼ yd. (1.1 m) of 55-in. (140-cm)-wide plain cotton fabric
- ¼ yd. (0.2 m) of 45-in. (115-cm)-wide floral cotton fabric
- 1¼ yd. (1.1 m) of ¼-in. (6-mm)-wide ribbon
- matching sewing thread

Note: The pillowcase fits a standard pillow measuring 30 x 20 in. (75 x 50 cm).

Cutting Out

Note: Seam allowances of ⅝ in. (1.5 cm) are included throughout unless otherwise stated.

From the main fabric, cut a 21¼ x 31¼-in. (54 x 79-cm) rectangle for the front and a 21¼ x 39⅞-in. (54 x 101-cm) rectangle for the back and inside flap. From the floral fabric, cut two 6 x 21¼-in. (15 x 54-cm) strips.

3 HOURS OR LESS

SEW PROJECT

Matching pillowcases give bed linens a very sophisticated look that is easy to achieve.

1 Pin the right side of a floral fabric strip to the wrong side of the front along one short edge of the front, then machine stitch them together. Turn the strip over to the right side and baste the raw edge to the right side of the front by hand. Pin a length of ribbon over the raw edge and topstitch it in place, stitching close to each edge.

2 Pin the wrong side of the other floral strip to the right side of the other end of the front, matching the raw edges and baste in place along the raw edges. Pin a length of ribbon over the inside raw edge and topstitch it in place as before.

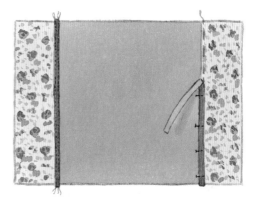

3 Turn under a hem of ¼ in. (6 mm) then ⅜ in. (1 cm) along one short edge of the back for the flap edge, and stitch. With right sides together, matching the edges, pin the front to the back so that the flap extends beyond the finished edge of the front by 8½ in. (22 cm). Fold the flap over the front and pin.

4 Machine stitch along three sides leaving the flap edge unstitched. Neaten the seams with a machine zigzag stitch. Turn the pillowcase right side out and press.

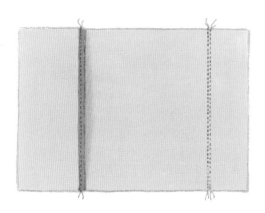

Floral bolster cover with tied ends

A bolster is a good shape for propping up other pillows and is especially useful for reading in bed. This pretty blue-and-white bolster cover with sprigs of country-style flowers is buttoned around the pillow form and has optional piping for a tailored finish. Use a lightweight cotton fabric, so that the drawstring ends don't become too bulky when they are tied.

1 To pipe the seams, prepare 1½ yd. (1.4 m) of piping (see page 155), or use purchased piping. Starting 1¾ in. (4 cm) from one end (the buttonhole-band edge), cut the piping in half and pin it to the right side of the center panel down both long edges, with the raw edges facing outward and the piping cord just inside the seam allowance. Finish 3 in. (7 cm) from the other end.

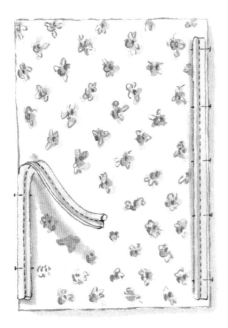

You Will Need

- 28¼ x 18¾ in. (72 x 48 cm) of cotton fabric for center panel
- 28¼ x 10 in. (72 x 26 cm) of cotton fabric in a contrasting color for the bolster ends
- 1½ yd. (1.4 m) of piping cord, or 12 x 16 in. (30 x 40 cm) cotton in the contrasting bolster end fabric (optional)
- four 1-in. (2.5-cm) buttons
- bolster pillow form 17½ in. (45 cm) long and 6¾ in. (17 cm) in diameter
- ¼ yd. (10 cm) of 36-in. (90-cm)-wide cotton fabric, or 2 yd. (1.8 m) of cord for the drawstrings
- matching sewing thread

Note: The bolster cover fits a pillow form 17½ in. (45 cm) long and 6¾ in. (17 cm) in diameter.

Cutting Out

Note: Seam allowances of ⅝ in. (1.5 cm) are included throughout unless otherwise stated.

Cut two 28¼ x 5-in. (72 x 13-cm) rectangles from the contrasting fabric for the bolster ends.

⏱ **3 HOURS OR LESS**

✂ **LOW-SEW PROJECT**

Mixing harmonious colors in the bolster gives a pretty effect.

2 With right sides together, pin the long edge of one bolster end piece to the long edge of the center panel, so that the piping is sandwiched in between. Using a zipper foot on the machine, sew the two pieces together. Stitch the other bolster end piece to the other side of the center panel in the same way.

3 Turn under ⅝ in. (1.5 cm) and then 1¼ in. (3.5 cm) along the whole length of the buttonhole-band edge, including the end pieces, and stitch in place from the wrong side, stitching as close to the turned-under edges as possible. Make the button band along the opposite edge in the same way, but turning under ⅝ in. (1.5 cm) and then 2¼ in. (6 cm).

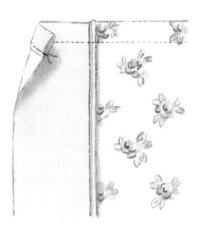

Positioning Buttons

■ To space buttons evenly, first work out how many buttons you need to use to hold the piece firmly closed.

■ Then count up the number of spaces between the buttons. If there are four buttons—as on this bolster, for example—there will be three spaces between them. Add one space at either end—so in this example, there will be five spaces in total.

■ Divide the total length of the piece by the total number of spaces and make a mark at each point, using a soft pencil or tailor's chalk. Sew a button to each marked point.

4 To make the drawstring casings, turn under ⅝ in. (1.5 cm) followed by another ¾ in. (2 cm) along the raw edge of each bolster end piece and press the folds. Open out the casings and make a ½-in. (12-mm) buttonhole on each side, just below and parallel to the buttonhole-band topstitching, to fit within the width of the casing. Topstitch the casings in place, leaving the ends open. Make four evenly spaced buttonholes along the buttonhole band within the center panel. Hand stitch one button along the button band to correspond to each buttonhole .

5 Cut two 35-in. (90-cm) lengths of cord or, following the instructions below, make two drawstrings 35 in. (90 cm) long, and thread them through the casings. Wrap the cover around the bolster pillow form, fasten the buttons, and pull the drawstrings to close the ends, tying in bows to complete.

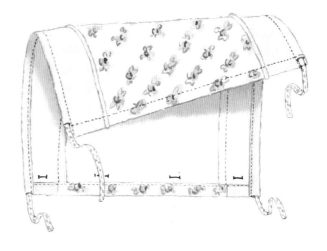

Professional's Tip: Making the Drawstrings

■ To make a drawstring ⅝ in. (1.5 cm) wide, cut two fabric strips 2 in. (5 cm) wide x 35 in. (88 cm) long.

■ Fold the strips in half lengthwise, right sides together, and sandwich a length of strong smooth cord ¼ in. (6 mm) in diameter in between.

■ Machine stitch along one short end to secure the cord, and sew down the length ⅝ in. (1.5 cm) from the fold, taking care not to catch the cord in the stitching.

■ Trim the seam, then turn the drawstring right side out by pulling the cord down through the middle. Cut off the end holding the cord. Turn under the raw edges of the fabric and work a few slip stitches to secure.

Below: Carefully sew the strip of fabric along the length of the cord.

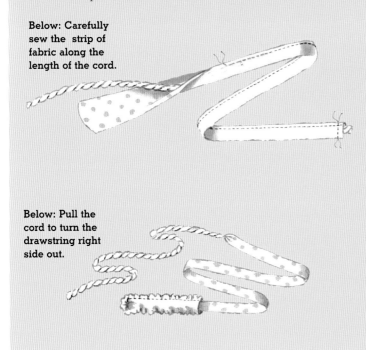

Below: Pull the cord to turn the drawstring right side out.

| Complement with... |

No-sew bolster cover

This elegant bolster cover doesn't even require any stitching; instead, iron-on fusible web is used to create the hems, and Velcro fasteners to close the cover around the pillow form. All you need to tie the ends in place are two lengths of ribbon.

You Will Need

- ⅞ yd. (0.8 cm) of 45-in. (115-cm)-wide cotton fabric
- 2¼ yd. (2 m) of ¾-in. (22-mm)-wide fusible web
- 1¾ yd. (1.5 m) of ⅜-in. (10-mm)-wide ribbon
- 1¾ yd. (1.5 m) of ⅜-in. (10-mm)-wide fusible web
- five stick-on Velcro pads
- bolster pillow form 17½ in. (45 cm) long and 6 ¾ in. (17 cm) in diameter
- 2 yd. (1.8 m) of 1½-in. (38-mm)-wide ribbon

Note: Seam allowances of ⅝ in. (1.5 cm) are included throughout unless otherwise stated.

Note: The bolster cover fits a pillow form 17½ in. (45 cm) long and 6 ¾ in. (17 cm) in diameter.

 3 HOURS OR LESS

 NO-SEW PROJECT

With lush roses and satin ribbon, this quick bolster is perfect for adding instant elegance.

1 Cut a 38 x 28-in. (97 x 72-cm) rectangle of fabric. Turn under and press a ¾-in. (2-cm) hem along each long edge. Following the manufacturer's instructions, secure the hems with ⅞-in. (22-mm)-wide fusible web.

2 Cut two 28-in. (72-cm) lengths of ⅜-in. (10-mm)-wide ribbon. Using ⅜-in. (10-mm)-wide fusible web, iron the ribbon in place to cover the raw edges at either end.

3 Mark the center 17½ in. (45 cm) point along one long side of the cover with a pin. Stick five Velcro pads to the wrong side of this edge, spacing them evenly on either side of the center point and leave to dry for a few minutes. Stick the other halves of the Velcro pads to the ones already in place. Fold this edge so that it overlaps the opposite edge, and the other halves of the Velcro pads will stick in place on the right side of the fabric. Leave the adhesive to dry for a few minutes before you pull the Velcro pads apart.

4 To make up the cover, wrap it around the bolster pillow form and secure with the Velcro pads. Cut two pieces of 1½-in.- (38-mm-) wide ribbon. Gather up the ends, tying them together with a bow, as shown at left on page 54.

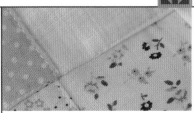

Country-style patchwork throw

This throw is made by stitching overlapping squares together—much easier and quicker than traditional patchwork. The charming, country-style fabrics give a look that has an heirloom quality but doesn't take an age to achieve. For accuracy and speed, it is well worth using a rotary cutter and cutting mat to cut several layers at once (see page 148). When stitching, measure the overlaps as accurately as possible, as a small discrepancy on each row will make a big difference over the whole width.

You Will Need

- ¾ yd. (0.7 m) 45-in. (115-cm)-wide cotton in each of four fabrics for the patchwork
- 1¾ yd. (1.6 m) of 55-in. (140-cm)-wide cotton fabric for the backing and border
- 1¾ yd. (1.6 m) of 55-in. (140-cm)-wide lightweight batting
- 24 ⅜-in. (1-cm) pearl buttons
- matching sewing thread

Note: The throw measures approximately 46 x 57 in. (117 x 145 cm).

Cutting Out

Note: Seam allowances of ⅝ in. (1.5 cm) are included throughout unless otherwise stated.

Cut 120 2⅞-in. (74-mm) squares each from fabrics 1 and 3, and 108 2⅞-in. (74-mm) squares each from fabrics 2 and 4.

 6 TO 8 HOURS

 SEW PROJECT

1 Press under ⅜ in. (1 cm) on one side of each of the squares. Take ten fabric 1 squares and nine fabric 2 squares and arrange them in a row with the folded edges on the right, alternating the fabrics. Place the folded edge of a fabric 1 square over the unfolded edge of a fabric 2 square, overlapping by ⅜ in. (1 cm). Pin and topstitch in place. Overlap, pin, and topstitch the folded edge of the fabric 2 square on the unfolded edge of the next fabric 1 square. Continue in this way until you have completed a strip of 19 squares. Make a second strip in the same way, using fabrics 3 and 4. Make 11 more pairs of strips.

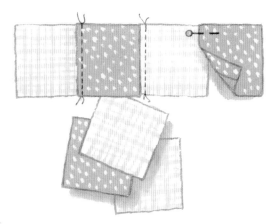

This throw is perfect for taking into the garden on days with a slight chill in the air.

2 Press under ⅜ in. (1 cm) along one long edge on each of the 24 strips. Overlap a strip 1 (comprising fabrics 1 and 2) on a strip 2 (comprising fabrics 3 and 4) by ⅜ in. (1 cm), matching the seamlines as closely as possible, and pin the strips together. Top-stitch to join the strips together. Continue joining the strips, alternating strips 1 and 2, until all 24 strips have been stitched together.

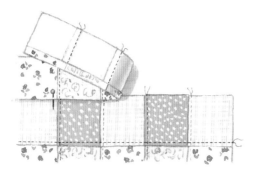

3 Measure the assembled patchwork. For the top and bottom borders, cut two strips 4¾ in. (12 cm) deep and 7 in. (18cm) wider than the patchwork. For the side borders, cut two strips 4¾ in. (12 cm) wide and 8 in. (20 cm) longer than the patchwork. On each of the four border strips, measure 4¾ in. (12 cm) in from each end along one long edge and mark with pins. (This will be the border inside edge.) Draw a diagonal pencil line from the pin marker to the outside corner on the wrong side of each strip.

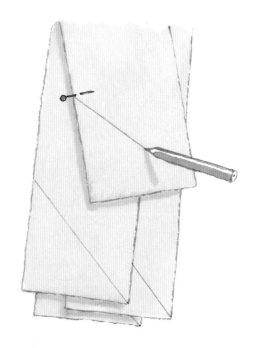

4 Right sides together, pin and machine stitch the border strips together along the marked lines, stopping ⅝ in. (1.5 cm) from the inner edge of each seam, together to form a rectangular frame with mitered corners. Trim the seam allowances and press open.

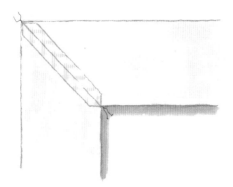

5 With right sides together, pin the inner edge of the border to the edges of the patchwork; the open part of each seam will allow the border to fit round the corner. Machine stitch. Turn the border right side out, and press.

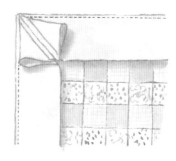

6 Lay the batting flat on a large table or clean floor with the backing fabric right side up on top of it. Place the patchwork right side down on the backing fabric and smooth all layers to get rid of any wrinkles. Working from the center outward, pin the layers together and cut away any excess batting and backing fabric. Machine stitch around all four sides, leaving a 16-in. (40-cm) opening in one side. Remove the pins.

7 Turn the throw right side out and press. Slip stitch the opening closed by hand (see page 149).

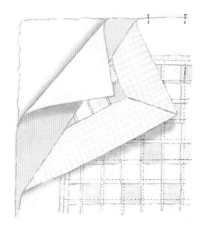

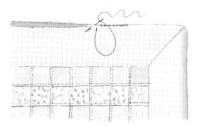

8 Working from the center outward, smooth the layers and insert pins at regular intervals, pinning through all three layers. Top stitch through all the layers along the edge of the border on the patchwork. Remove the pins.

9 Sew a button at each corner of the patchwork on the inside edge of the miter. Sew five rows of four buttons across the patchwork, placing them where squares intersect and spacing them evenly, stitching through all layers.

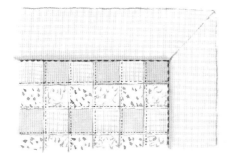

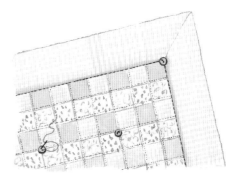

Professional's Tip: Style alternative

This patchwork design offers great scope for variations to suit different settings.
■ Using solid-colored fabric makes topstitching more conspicuous. Make a feature of it by using buttonhole twist or a glossy machine embroidery thread in the needle.

Lavender pillow

Lavender is a highly aromatic plant that has been valued for centuries for its calming and relaxing properties as well as for more practical reasons. A lavender-filled pillow placed in a linen closet, for example, not only keeps the linens sweet and scented, but also wards off insects. This lavender pillow, with its floral pattern and dainty bow, is too lovely to be hidden away, so arrange it with other pillows on a bed and let the delicious aroma tempt you to sleep. A panel of semi-transparent fabric down the center—cotton or silk organdy, or a printed cotton voile or muslin—allows you to glimpse the floral mixture inside.

You Will Need

- 10 x 20-in. (25 x 50-cm) piece of cotton fabric
- 8 x 4-in. (20 x 10-cm) piece of cotton organdy for the center panel
- 1 yd. (90 cm) length of ⅜-in. (10-mm)-wide ribbon
- 1¼ yd. (1 m) of ⅛-in. (3-mm) piping cord and a 9 x 11-in. (23 x 28-cm) piece of fabric to make the piping or 1¼ yd. (1 m) purchased piping
- 7 oz. (200 g) dried lavender flowers
- matching sewing thread

Note: The pillow measures 8 in. (20 cm) square.

Cutting Out

Note: Seam allowances of ⅝ in. (1.5 cm) are included throughout. unless otherwise stated.

From the cotton fabric, cut a 9¼-in. (23-cm) square for the back, two 3⅞ x 9¼-in. (9.5 x 23-cm) rectangles for the front side panels, and two 1⅞ x 4-in. (4.5 x 10-cm) rectangles to edge the center panel.

Cut bias strips 1⅝ in. (4 cm) wide to make bias binding and make up 1 yd. (1 m) of piping (see page 155).

 3 HOURS OR LESS

 SEW PROJECT

The soft blues and mauves of the fabric enhance the color of the dried lavender flowers.

1 With right sides together, pin one long edge of an edge rectangle to a short edge of the cotton organdy center panel and machine stitch. Trim the seam and press toward the edge rectangle. Stitch the other edge rectangle to the other short edge of the center panel in the same way.

2 With wrong sides together, pin the long edge of a side panel to the center panel and machine stitch. Trim the seam and press toward the side panel. Stitch the other side panel to the other side of the center panel in the same way. Cut two lengths of ribbon the same length as the seam. Pin one on each side of the center panel and topstitch in place, stitching close to the ribbon edges.

3 Pin the piping around the edge of the right side of the pillow front, clipping the raw edges of the fabric to turn the corners and joining the ends where they meet (see page 155). Baste in place. With right sides together, pin the front and back of the pillow together and machine stitch around all four sides, leaving a 3-in. (7-cm) gap in one side.

4 Trim the seam, turn the pillow right side out, and press. Make a bow from the remaining ribbon and handstitch it onto one of the ribbon stripes. Fill the pillow with dried lavender and slip stitch the opening closed.

Pillowcase with buttons

When you make your own pillowcases, you are not limited to using the extra-wide fabrics normally used to make bed linen: you can choose from a larger selection of cotton dress fabrics and make pillowcases to coordinate with duvet covers and sheets, and even curtains. This standard pillowcase is made from a delicate cotton fabric with tiny sprigs of flowers. It has a border in a solid color that complements the flower pattern and is finished with three buttons covered in the same cotton fabric.

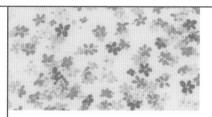

You Will Need
- ¾ yd. (0.6 m) of 60-in. (150-cm)-wide cotton print for main fabric
- ⅜ yd. (0.3 m) 45-in. (115-cm)-wide solid cotton fabric for the button border
- three 1-in. (2.5-cm) buttons to cover and matching cotton thread

Note: The pillowcase fits a standard pillow measuring 30 x 20 in. (75 x 50 cm).

Cutting Out
Note: Seam allowances of ⅝ in. (1.5 cm) are included throughout unless otherwise stated.

Cut two 29¼ x 21¼-in. (74 x 53-cm) rectangles from the main fabric for the front and back, and two 9¼ x 21¼-in. (23 x 53-cm) rectangles from the border fabric.

⏱ 3 HOURS OR LESS

🪡 LOW-SEW PROJECT

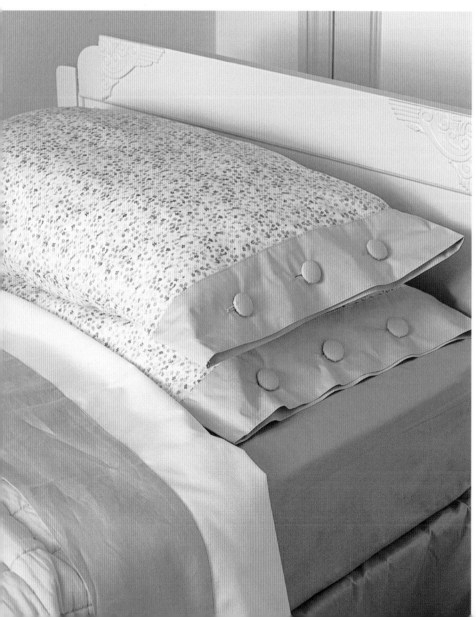

Dainty floral patterns in crisp cotton are ideal for brightening plain bedding.

1 With right sides together, pin a long edge of one border piece to a short edge of a main piece and machine stitch. Press the seam toward the border. Join the second border piece to the other main piece in the same way.

2 Right sides together, pin the front and back together aligning the border seams. Machine stitch along three sides, leaving the border edge open. Press the border seams and the next 2 in. (5 cm) of the main pieces open. Neaten the seams with machine zigzag stitch.

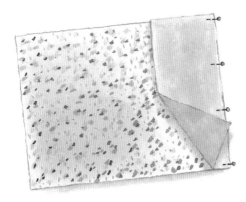

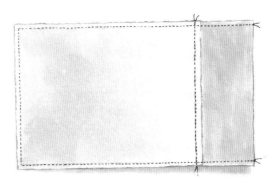

3 Press under the seam allowance along the border edge and trim the seam allowance to ½ in. (1 cm). Fold the border in half, so that the turned-under edge meets the seam on the wrong side of the pillowcase, and slip stitch in place. Topstitch from the right side close to both edges of the border. Press flat.

4 Make three evenly spaced buttonholes along the front border (see pages 151–152), 2 in. (5 cm) in from the outer edge of the border. Cover the buttons in the border fabric (see page 153) and hand stitch them to the inside of the back border to correspond with the buttonholes.

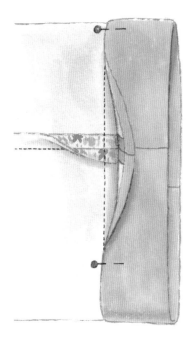

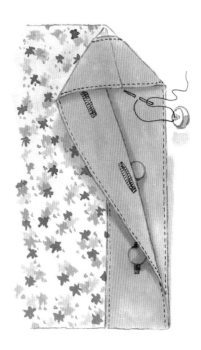

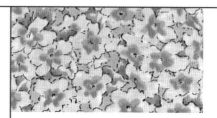

Complement with...

Pillowcase with lace trim

Here the fabrics are reversed, with a print fabric forming the border and a solid color the main area of the pillowcase. This variation omits the buttons but features a strip of lace trim set into the seam—a professional-looking finish that resembles hand embroidery. To complete the look, finish the top edge of a flat sheet with a matching band of the print fabric.

You Will Need

- 1¼ yd. (1.1 m) 45-in. (115-cm)-wide solid cotton for main fabric
- ⅜ yd. (0.3 m) 36-in. (90-cm)-wide cotton print fabric for the contrasting border
- 22-in. (54-cm) of lace trim
- matching cotton thread

Note: The pillowcase fits a standard pillow measuring 30 x 20 in. (75 x 50 cm).

Cutting Out

Note: Seam allowances of ⅝ in. (1.5 cm) are included throughout unless otherwise stated.

From the main fabric, cut a 27¼ x 21¼-in. (68 x 53-cm) rectangle for the front and a 39½ x 21¼-in. (99 x 53-cm) rectangle for the back. From the print border fabric, cut a 9¼ x 21¼-in. (23 x 53-cm) rectangle.

 3 HOURS OR LESS

LOW-SEW PROJECT

The edging fabric used here accents the bright color of the existing coverlet.

1 With wrong sides together, fold the border in half lengthwise and press. Machine zigzag stitch along the long raw edges. Zigzag one short edge of the front piece, fold under the seam allowance to the wrong side, and press.

2 Pin the lace trim along the middle of the seam-line on the front of the border and baste it in place by hand. Pin the turned edge of the front piece over the trim so that the fold meets the seamline along the middle of the trim. Topstitch it in place.

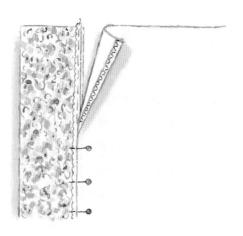

3 Turn under ⅜ in. (1 cm), followed by a ⅝-in. (1.5-cm) hem along one short edge of the back border piece for the inside flap edge, and machine stitch. With right sides together, pin the back and front together, matching the short raw edges, so that the inside flap extends beyond the front border edge.

4 Fold the flap over the wrong side of the front and pin. Stitch along three sides, leaving the inside flap of the border edge open. Machine zigzag stitch the seams. Turn the pillowcase right side out and press.

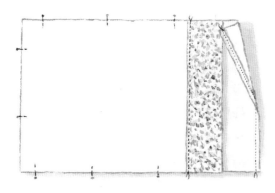

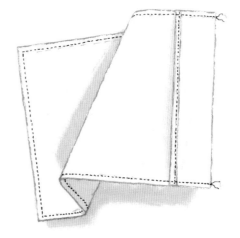

Child's bed linen set

Flower motifs in pastel shades are a charming embellishment for a child's duvet cover. The motifs are applied using fusible bonding web, which makes it easy to cut out the shapes without the fabric fraying.

You Will Need

- 5¾ yd. (5.2 m) of 55-in. (140-cm)-wide cotton fabric
- fusible bonding web
- seven x ¾-in. (2-cm) buttons
- matching sewing thread

For the flowers:

- 9½ x 7½ in. (24 x 18 cm) piece of pink cotton fabric
- 11½ x 6½ in. (29 x 16 cm) piece of peach cotton fabric
- 9½ x 5½ in. (24 x 13 cm) piece of yellow cotton fabric

Note: The cover fits a standard children's duvet measuring 53½ x 80 in. (135 x 200 cm).

 6 TO 8 HOURS

 SEW PROJECT

Daisylike flowers will be adored by little girls. For boys use fish or animal motifs instead.

1 Arrange the flower motifs in rows on the right side of one of the turn-back pieces, alternating the colors and spacing them evenly in rows of the same size and type, and avoiding seam allowances. Remove the backing from the fusible bonding web on each flower, cover with a damp cloth, and iron in place following the manufacturer's instructions. Using matching thread, zigzag around the edge of each flower and stitch a small block of stitches at the center of each flower.

2 With right sides together, fold one of the ties in half lengthwise and stitch along one short edge and down the long side. Trim the seam and turn the tie right side out. With the seam running down the side edge, press the tie flat. Make three more ties in the same way.

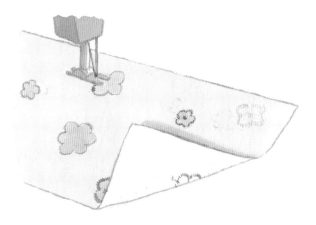

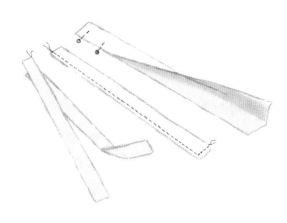

Cutting Out

Note: Seam allowances of ⅝ in. (1.5 cm) are included throughout unless otherwise stated.

From the main fabric, cut two 54¾ x 82-in. (139 x 205-cm) rectangles for the back and front, a 54¾ x 10-in. (139 x 26-cm) strip for the inside flap, two 13 x 54¾-in. (33 x 139-cm) rectangles for the turn-back, and four 15 x 2¾-in. (38 x 7-cm) rectangles for the side ties.

Iron fusible bonding web to the wrong side of the fabrics for the flower petals. Enlarge the motifs below to 200% and trace them onto card. Using a dress-maker's pencil, draw around the card patterns on the wrong side of the fabrics, and cut:

For the duvet cover: Small four-petaled flowers: 3 pink, 3 yellow;

Small six-petaled flowers: 3 pink, 3 peach;

Large four-petaled flowers: 3 peach, 3 yellow;

Large six-petaled flowers: 3 pink, 3 peach.

For the pillowcase:

Large four-petaled flowers: 2 peach, 1 yellow;

Large six-petaled flowers: 1 pink, 1 peach.

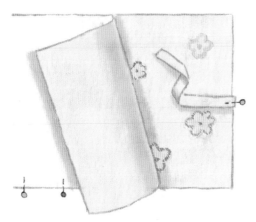

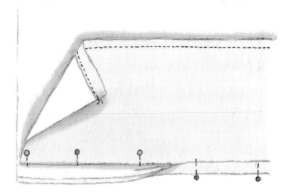

3 Pin a tie to the middle of each short edge on the right side of the turn-back with the stitched flowers, keeping the raw edges together. With right sides together, pin the two turn-back pieces together and machine stitch along both short edges and one long edge. Trim the seam, turn right side out, and press. Baste the raw edges together.

4 Turn under a hem of ⅜ in. (1 cm) followed by ¾ in. (2 cm) along one long edge of the inside flap, and machine stitch. With wrong sides together, pin the flap to the bottom edge of the duvet cover back so that the long raw edge is 2 in. (5 cm) up from the bottom edge. Turn under a hem of ⅜ in. (1 cm) followed by 1 in. (2.5 cm) along the bottom edge of the duvet cover back, so that the folded edge overlaps the raw edge of the flap by ⅜ in. (1 cm), and machine stitch close to the turned-under edge to make the button band. Turn under a hem of ⅜ in. (1 cm) followed by 1 in. (2.5 cm) along the bottom edge of the cover front and machine stitch to make the buttonhole band.

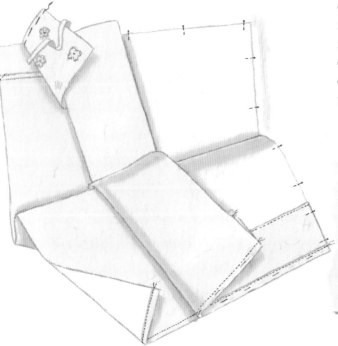

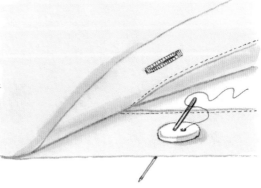

5 Make seven evenly spaced buttonholes along the buttonhole band (see pages 151–152). Pin a tie to each side edge on the right side of the front, 6½ in. (16.5 cm) down from the top edge, matching raw edges. Right sides together and the flower side down, pin the turn-back along the top edge of the front, matching raw edges and aligning the finished side edges of the turn-back with the side seamline. With right sides together, join the front and back along both long edges and the top short edge, machine stitching through all four layers.

6 Neaten the seams with a machine zigzag stitch, turn the cover right side out, and press. Sew buttons along the inside of the button band to correspond with each buttonhole. Fasten the ties in bows along the side edges to hold the turn-back in place.

Complement with...

Matching pillowcase *The same machine-embroidered flower motifs are used to decorate the matching pillowcase with ties fastening into bows. If you are doing machine embroidery for the first time, this pillowcase would be a good starting point.*

You Will Need

- 1¼ yd. (1.1 m) of 55-in. (140-cm)-wide cotton fabric
- fusible bonding web
- matching sewing thread

For the flowers:

- 3½-in. (8-cm) square of pink cotton fabric
- 3½-in. (8-cm) square of yellow cotton fabric
- 9½ x 3½ in. (24 x 8 cm) piece of peach cotton fabric

Note: The pillowcase fits a standard pillow measuring 30 x 20 in. (75 x 50 cm).

Cutting Out

Note: Seam allowances of ⅝ in. (1.5 cm) are included throughout unless otherwise stated.

From the main fabric, cut two 31¼ x 21¼-in. (73 x 53-cm) rectangles for the front and back, one 7½ x 21¼-in. (19 x 53-cm) rectangle for the front border, one 10 x 21¼-in. (25.5 x 53-cm) rectangle for the inside flap, and four 15 x 2¾-in. (38 x 7-cm) rectangles for the ties.

3 HOURS OR LESS

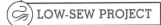
LOW-SEW PROJECT

1 Stitch the flowers to the right side of the border as for the duvet cover (see page 67, step 1), and make four ties (see page 67, step 2). Pin two ties to the wrong side of one short edge of the pillow front, then pin the right side of the border to the wrong side of the same pillow front edge. Stitch, turn the border to the right side, and press. Fold under ⅜ in. (1 cm) to the wrong side along the raw long border edge, then topstitch in place on the pillowcase front.

2 Turn under a hem of ⅜ in. (1 cm), followed by ⅝ in. (1.5 cm) along one long edge of the inside flap, and stitch. Pin two ties to the right side of a back short edge. With right sides together, pin the flap to the back along the tie edge and stitch. Pin the pillow front and back right sides together and fold the right side of the flap over the wrong side of the pillow front. Stitch along three sides of the pillowcase. Neaten the seams with a zigzag stitch.

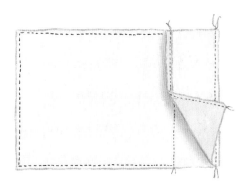

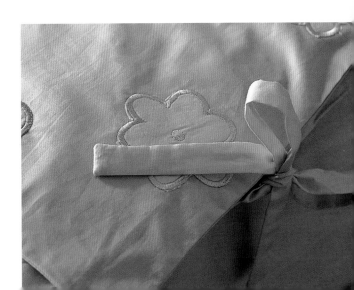

chapter three

TABLE LINENS

Brighten up your kitchen, dining room, and even patio tables with this easy-to-make collection of tablecloths and table accessories, along with decorative runners for everyday and special occasions.

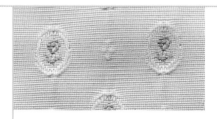

Padded place mat

Place mats are an important element for dressing a table. This softly padded mat, trimmed with sparkling beads and satin ribbon, looks incredibly luxurious. For informal dining, make each mat different; for more formal occasions, make a matching set.

You Will Need

- 17¼ x 13½ in. (44 x 34 cm) piece of fabric for the place mat front
- 17¼ x 13½ in. (44 x 34 cm) piece of fabric for the place mat back
- 17¼ x 13½ in. (44 x 34 cm) piece of interlining or thin cotton batting
- 27 in. (68 cm) length of ¼-in. (6-mm)-wide ribbon in each of two colors
- 26 in. (66 cm) beaded trim
- matching polycotton thread

Note: Seam allowances of ⅝ in. (1.5 cm) are included throughout unless otherwise stated.

Note: The place mat measures 16 x 12¼ in. (41 x 31 cm).

3 HOURS OR LESS

LOW-SEW PROJECT

Coordinate the colors of the beaded trim with your fabric for a stylish finish.

1 Cut each piece of ribbon in half. Pin one length of the first color down each short edge of the place mat front, 1½ in. (4 cm) from the edge. Pin the lengths of the second color ¼ in. (6 mm) away from the first ones. Top stitch along both edges of each ribbon.

2 Press the seam allowance to the wrong side along the short edges of the place mat front and back. Trim ¾ in. (2 cm) from each short edge of the interlining. Lay the place mat front right side down on a flat surface, center the interlining on top, and fold over the pressed seam allowances. Baste by hand to hold in place.

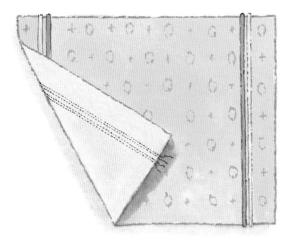

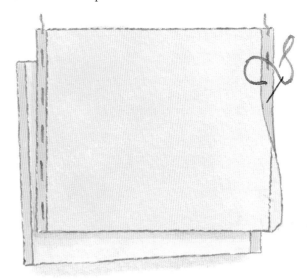

3 With right sides together, pin the front of the place mat to the back and machine stitch along both long edges. Trim the seams to ¼ in. (6 mm). Turn the place mat right side out and press.

4 Pin the short edges closed and baste. Cut the beaded trim to fit along both short edges and pin it in place along the short edges of the front of the place mat, turning the ends under. Topstitch in place, stitching through all layers. Remove the basting stitches.

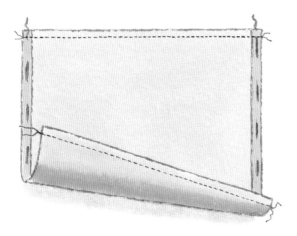

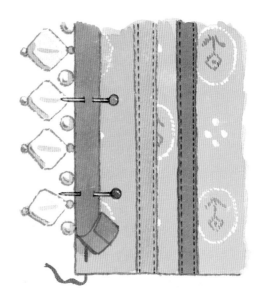

Complement with...

Oval place mat
This classic oval place mat has a contemporary twist with bright splashes of pink and turquoise. A soft layer of interlining makes the mat more substantial and protects the tabletop from heat and scratches.

You Will Need
- pattern paper and pencil
- 16 x 12¼-in. (41 x 31-cm) rectangle in the place mat top fabric, backing fabric, and thin cotton batting or interlining
- 12 x 9-in. (30 x 23-cm) piece of the backing fabric to make the binding
- matching polycotton thread

Note: The place mat measures 16 x 12¼ in. (41 x 31 cm).

Cutting Out
Note: Seam allowances of ⅝ in. (1.5 cm) are included throughout unless otherwise stated.

Draw a 16 x 12¼-in. (41 x 31-cm) rectangle on paper and fold it in half, bringing the short edges together. Open out, and with the fold at the center, place a small plate flat at either end over the center fold, draw matching curves on the two outer corners, and cut out. Using this pattern piece, cut out the place mat front, interlining, and backing.

 3 HOURS OR LESS

 **LOW-SEW PROJECT**

Left: An oval mat is ideal to use in the center of the table for hot serving dishes.

1 Place the backing fabric right side down on a flat surface, with the interlining on top and the front piece right side up on top of the interlining. Smooth the pieces flat and make sure the edges of all pieces align. Baste together by hand around the edges.

2 Cut 2-in. (5-cm)-wide bias strips from the backing fabric, joining them (see page 154) to make a 55-in. (140-cm) continuous length. Press open the seams.

3 Press under ½ in. (1.2 cm) along one edge of the binding. With the right side of the binding to the wrong side of the place mat, pin the raw edge of the binding all around the mat, cutting away any excess and joining the ends when they meet (see page 155). Machine stitch.

4 Fold the binding to the front of the mat and fold under ½ in. (1.2 cm) to meet the line of machine stitching. Pin and baste in place. Topstitch the binding on the right side, close to the turned-under edge, and press. Remove the basting stitches.

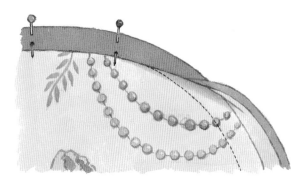

Professional's Tip: Bias-Binding Maker

You can purchase a tool to make bias binding quickly and easily; ask your local sewing-machine retailer for information. Be sure to follow the particular device's instructions for strips of the correct width; the devices range from those that produce strips of ¼ in. (6 mm) through 1 in. (2.5 cm) wide. For bias strips folded to ½ in. (1.2 cm) wide, cut strips 1 in (2.5 cm) wide.

■ Cut a diagonal strip of fabric, slip into the wide end of the binding maker, and press the neatly folded end of the binding while pulling it through.

Frayed linen tablecloth

This stylish tablecloth exploits the natural, even weave of the linen, the cloth's edges being frayed all around to make an attractive fringed border. A line of braid prevents the cloth from fraying any further, while frayed patches sewn around the edges of the cloth continue the theme. Table linen needs to be laundered regularly, so wash the fabric before you begin and always iron it when it is slightly damp, flattening the fringe to keep it looking neat.

You Will Need

- 2¼ yd. (2.1 m) of 60-in. (150-cm)-wide linen
- 6 in. (15 cm) of 60-in. (150-cm)-wide linen in each of two contrasting colors
- 7¾ yd. (7 m) of ½-in. (12-mm)-wide braid
- matching sewing thread

Note: The tablecloth measures 80 x 58 in. (204 x 147 cm).

Cutting Out

Using the full width of the fabric, cut an 80-in. (204-cm) length of fabric, following a thread in each direction to get straight edges along the grain of the fabric. Cut off the selvage on both sides, again following the grain of the fabric. Cut ten 5¾-in. (14-cm) squares from each of the contrasting fabrics, following the grain of the fabric.

3 HOURS OR LESS

LOW-SEW PROJECT

The slubby texture of linen, that shows best in pale colors, suits informal summer dining.

1 Using a needle to tease out the threads, pull out warp and weft threads one by one to fray the edges and make a fringe 1 in. (2.5 cm) deep on all four sides of the tablecloth.

2 Pin the braid around all four sides of the cloth on the inside edge of the fringe, mitering the corners (see page 83). Overlap the ends where they meet, and topstitch in place.

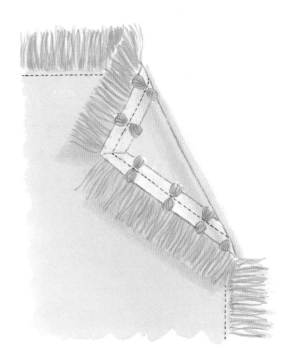

3 Fray the edges of each of the 5¾-in. (14-cm) squares to a depth of ⅝ in. (1.5 cm) on all four sides. Alternating the colors, space the patches evenly around the outer edge of the tablecloth, so that there are five patches along each short edge of the cloth and seven along each long edge. Place them at different angles and pin them in place.

4 Machine stitch the patches in place, stitching along the inside edge of the fringe. Push up the fringe around the patches so that it stands away from the cloth slightly.

Complement with...

Matching Napkin

On the napkin, a small fringed square decorates each corner to coordinate with the larger patches on the tablecloth. Fine satin ribbon finishes off the edges and stops the fabric from fraying.

You Will Need

- 22-in. (56-cm) square of linen
- 3½-in. (9-cm) square of linen in a contrasting color
- 2½ yd. (2.25 m) of ¼-in. (8-mm)-wide ribbon
- matching sewing thread

Note: Each napkin is 22 in. (56 cm) square.

 3 HOURS OR LESS

 LOW-SEW PROJECT

Simply folded, these napkins complete a stylish place setting.

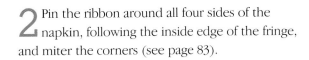

1 Fray the edges of the napkin to a depth of ¾ in. (2 cm) by pulling away the threads to make a fringed border.

2 Pin the ribbon around all four sides of the napkin, following the inside edge of the fringe, and miter the corners (see page 83).

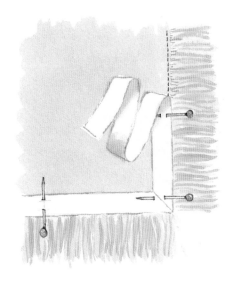

3 Topstitch the ribbon in place with matching sewing thread, stitching close to both edges.

4 Fray the edges of the contrasting-colored square on all four sides to a depth of ⅝ in. (1.5 cm) and pin the square at an angle inside one corner of the napkin. Stitch it in place, topstitching along the inside edge of the fringe.

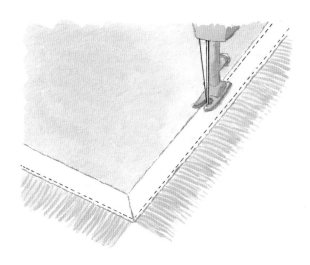

Table runner with beaded trim

A runner draped down the center of a table makes a stylish accessory. Place vases of flowers, candlesticks, and serving dishes across the runner and allow the ends to overhang by the same amount at each side. Sew beaded trim onto the ends to give more weight to the runner. This runner is cut out across the width of the fabric—but if your fabric has an obvious lengthwise pattern, cut it out in the other direction and piece together as necessary.

You Will Need

- ¾ yd. (0.6 m) of 55-in. (140-cm)-wide home decorating fabric (plus the depth of one pattern repeat length if needed)
- ¾ yd. (0.6 m) of 55-in. (140-cm)-wide lining
- 6½ yd. (5.8 m) of ½-in. (12-mm)-wide satin ribbon
- 30 in. (76 cm) beaded trim
- matching sewing thread

Note: The runner measures 10¾ x 107 in. (27 x 270 cm). Adjust to fit the size of your own table.

Cutting Out

Note: Seam allowances of ⅝ in. (1.5 cm) are included throughout unless otherwise stated.

From the main fabric, cut two strips 12 in. (30 cm) wide across the full width of the fabric, cutting the second strip so that the pattern aligns with the first one. Cut two strips the same size from the lining fabric.

LENGTH OF OVERHANG
Adjust the length of the strips at this point to fit your own table. Cut two strips the same size from the lining fabric.

3 HOURS OR LESS

LOW-SEW PROJECT

Rich colors and luxuriant fabrics make this runner perfect for a centerpiece display.

1 Fold one of the main fabric strips in half lengthwise. Draw a line from the fold to a point on the raw edge about 4 in. (10 cm) down from the end and cut along the line to form a gently angled point. Cut one end of the other main fabric strip and one end of each lining piece to match.

2 With right sides together, pin the straight short ends of the two main fabric strips together and machine stitch. Press the seam open. Join the two lining strips in the same way.

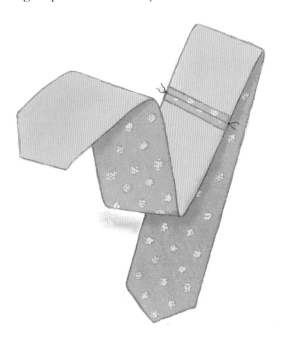

3 Pin the beaded trim to the right side of the slanted ends of the main piece, with the beads facing the center, just inside the seamline. Baste in place. With right sides together, pin the lining to the main piece, aligning the edges. Machine stitch all sides, leaving an 8-in. (20-cm) opening in one side.

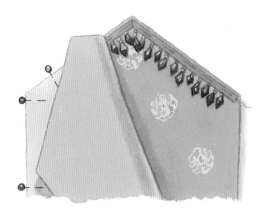

4 Trim the seam, turn right side out, and press the edges. Slip stitch the opening closed. Pin the ribbon to the right side of the main fabric along all sides ¼ in. (6 mm) in from the edges, folding the ribbon to make miters at each corner. Topstitch close to both edges of the ribbon.

Complement with...

Table runner with tassels

A tassel at each corner makes a novel embellishment, and a satin-ribbon border emphasizes the cream color in the fabric. For summer dining, use a pastel floral fabric to reflect the mood of the season.

You Will Need

- ¾ yd. (0.6 m) of 55-in. (140-cm)-wide home decorating fabric (plus the depth of one pattern repeat if needed)
- ¾ yd. (0.6 m) of 55-inch (140-cm)-wide lining
- 6⅝ yd. (6 m) of 1-in. (2.5-cm)-wide satin ribbon
- 4 tassels
- matching polycotton thread

Note: The runner measures 10¾ x 107 in. (27 x 270 cm).

Cutting Out

Note: Seam allowances of ⅝ in. (1.5 cm) are included throughout unless otherwise stated.

From the main fabric, cut two strips 12 in. (30 cm) wide across the full width of the fabric, cutting the second strip so that the pattern aligns with the first one. Adjust the length of the strips at this point to fit your own table; most overhangs hang about 6 in. (15 cm) from the edge of the table. Cut two strips the same size from the lining fabric.

 3 HOURS OR LESS

 LOW-SEW PROJECT

Tassels add weight to help the ends of a runner hang elegantly over the table. Fringed or beaded tassels would work well, too.

1 With right sides together, pin the main fabric strips together along one short edge and machine stitch. Press the seam open. Join the two lining strips in the same way. Pin a tassel to each corner of the main fabric, with the tassels facing inward, and baste in place by hand. With right sides together, pin the lining to the main piece, aligning the edges, and machine stitch along all sides, leaving an 8-in. (20-cm) opening along the middle of one side.

2 Trim the seam, turn the runner right side out, press the edges, and slip stitch the opening closed. Pin the ribbon to the right side of the main fabric along all sides ⅜ in. (1 cm) in from the edges, mitering the corners (see below). Topstitch along both edges of the ribbon.

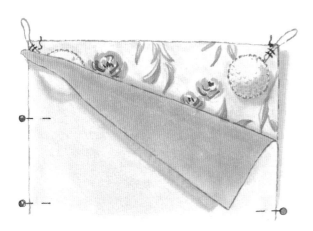

Professional's Tip: Applying Trim

When applying ribbon or braid trimming, take extra care in positioning it.
■ Work on a well-padded ironing board.
■ Start positioning the ribbon or braid in the center of one long side of the piece. Continue along this side, holding the ribbon or braid with pins placed vertically into the padded surface. When you reach the outer corner, fold the ribbon or braid straight back on itself, and press this fold. Place a pin at the outer corner, then turn the ribbon or braid at a 90° angle to follow the adjacent edge, thus forming a miter; press.
■ At this point, remove the vertical pins and re-insert them horizontally through the fabric layers. Continue along each following side as above. On reaching the starting point, turn under and trim the end of the ribbon or braid and pin it over the first end. Baste and topstitch in place.

Butterfly tablecloth

The sight of butterflies fluttering among the blooms of a flower border is one of the visual delights of the summer months. Here, embroidered butterfly motifs are incorporated into the design of a floral tablecloth that is perfect for *al fresco* summer dining. It can be expensive to buy ready-made motifs in large quantities, so arrange them close to the corners of the cloth, allowing just one or two to stray a little farther afield.

You Will Need

- 1¾ yd. (1.6 m) of 55-in. (140-cm)-wide floral cotton fabric
- 1¾ yd. (1.6 m) of 55-in. (140-cm)-wide solid-colored cotton fabric for the border
- 5¼ yd. (4.8 m) of ⅝-in. (15-mm)-wide ribbon
- a selection of embroidered butterfly motifs
- matching sewing thread

Note: The tablecloth measures approximately 61¾ x 53 in. (157 x 134 cm).

Cutting Out

Note: Seam allowances of ⅝ in. (1.5 cm) are included throughout unless otherwise stated.

From the floral fabric, cut a 63 x 54¼-in. (160 x 137-cm) rectangle for the tablecloth center. From the border fabric, cut two 54¼ x 6⅜-in. (137 x 16-cm) strips for the top and bottom borders and two 63 x 6⅜-in. (160 x 16-cm) strips for the side borders.

( ) 3 HOURS OR LESS

LOW-SEW PROJECT

Embellishing a tablecloth with motifs creates a very personal, charming effect.

1 On each of the four border strips, measure 6⅜ in. (16 cm) in from each end along one long edge and mark with pins. (This will be the border inside edge.) On the wrong side of the fabric, draw a diagonal pencil line from the pin marker to the outside corner on each strip.

2 With right sides together, pin together the short edges of one side border and the top border strip and machine stitch along the pencil line. Trim the seam and press it open. Join the bottom border to the other end of the side strip in the same way, and then join the remaining side strip between the top and bottom strips to form a rectangular frame with mitered corners.

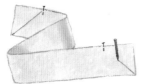

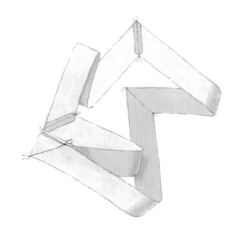

3 Pin the right side of the border to the wrong side of the fabric for the center of the tablecloth, matching the raw edges. Machine stitch around all four sides. Trim the seam, then fold the border over to the right side of the tablecloth center. Press and baste it in place by hand along the raw edge.

4 Pin the ribbon over the raw edge of the border all around the cloth, mitering it at the corners (see page 83), and topstitch it in place. Pin the motifs in position on the cloth, arranging them in groups in the corners among the flowers of the pattern. Stitch them in place.

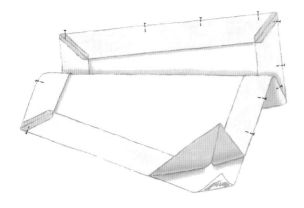

Complement with ...

Butterfly napkin ring

Butterflies similar to those used on the tablecloth can be used to make matching napkin rings. The wings are allowed to stand proud of the cloth, making it look as if the butterflies have landed fleetingly on the napkins. A strip of embroidered ribbon, with a pattern of roses and leaves, adds further embellishment and complements the floral theme of the tablecloth.

You Will Need

- 9¾ x 6½-in. (24 x 16-cm) piece of cotton fabric left over from the tablecloth border
- 10-in. (24-cm) length of 1⅛-in. (27-mm)-wide ribbon
- one stick-on Velcro pad
- one embroidered butterfly motif
- matching sewing thread

Note: The napkin ring measures approximately 8½ x 2 in. (21 x 5 cm) when opened out and makes a ring 2 in. (5 cm) in diameter when fastened.

Cutting Out

Note: Seam allowances of ⅝ in. (1.5 cm) are included throughout unless otherwise stated.

Fold the fabric in half lengthwise and cut along the fold.

🕐 **3 HOURS OR LESS**

✂ **LOW-SEW PROJECT**

These delightful butterflies are sure to charm guests at a summer garden party.

1 Pin the ribbon lengthwise along the center of the right side of one of the strips of fabric and topstitch it in place along both long edges. With right sides together, pin the front and back strips together and stitch along all four sides, leaving a 3-in. (7-cm) opening in one long edge. Trim the seam and corners, and turn the napkin ring right side out. Slip stitch the opening closed and press.

2 Pin the body of the butterfly motif 1 in. (2.5 cm) in from one end of the band. Topstitch it in place down each side of the body, so that the wings are free. Roll the band into a ring and stick one half of the Velcro pad to the wrong side, under the butterfly, and the other half to the right side of the other end of the band to hold it closed. Allow the adhesive to dry thoroughly before opening the pads.

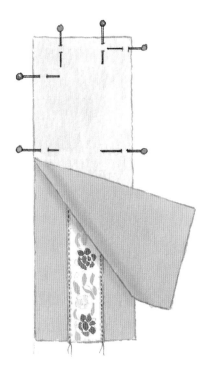

Professional's Tip: Making Motifs

You can adapt the idea shown here to use motifs cut from printed fabric.
■ First cut out the motif, leaving a small margin of fabric around it. Apply thin iron-on interfacing to the wrong side, then cut around the motif precisely. Pin and baste it to the background fabric, and stitch, using closed-up zigzag or hand buttonhole stitch.
■ For a free-standing motif, as on the napkin rings, apply the loosely cut-out motif to a solid-colored backing fabric, using fusible web. Then either zigzag-stitch around it and trim close to the stitching or cut first and finish the edges with buttonhole stitch.

chapter four

PILLOWS AND COVERS

Decorative pillows and covers are the simplest and quickest way of brightening up chairs and sofas. In this chapter you will find ideas to suit all styles and tastes.

Tasseled pillow with silk center panel

A strip of solid-colored silk, trimmed with bands of ribbon, forms the center panel of this pillow, contrasting beautifully with the elaborate fleur-de-lis fabric on either side. The center panel is small, so it's a great place for making the most of a piece of exquisite silk or embroidered upholstery fabric.

You Will Need
- ½ yd. (0.4 m) of 54-in. (136-cm) -wide home decorating fabric
- 5¼ x 13¼-in. (14 x 33-cm) rectangle of silk or other home decorating fabric for the center panel
- ¾-yd. (0.7 m) of 1-in. (2.5-cm) -wide ribbon or braid
- 10-in. (25-cm) zipper
- 4 tassels
- 12 x 16-in. (30 x 40-cm) pillow form
- matching polycotton thread

Note: The pillow measures 12 x 16 in. (30 x 40 cm).

Cutting Out
Note: Seam allowances of ⅝ in. (1.5 cm) are included throughout unless otherwise stated.

Cut two 13¼ x 7¼-in. (33 x 17.5-cm) rectangles of upholstery fabric for the pillow front and two 17¼ x 7¼ in. (43 x 18 cm) rectangles of home decorating fabric for the pillow back.

 3 HOURS OR LESS

 LOW-SEW PROJECT

Tassels are the perfect vintage embellishment for rich, traditional-style fabrics.

1 With right sides together, pin the two pillow back rectangles together along one long edge and mark 3⅝ in. (9 cm) in from each end with pins. Machine stitch up to the pins from each end. Now machine baste the center 10 in. (25 cm). Press the seam open.

2 Pin the zipper into the basted part of the seam and hand baste it in place. Using a zipper foot on the machine, stitch the zipper in place from the right side (see pageS 150–151). Remove the hand and machine basting. Open the zipper.

3 With right sides together, pin a long edge of one front piece to a long edge of the silk center panel and machine stitch. Pin and stitch the other front piece to the opposite side of the center panel in the same way. Press the seams open. Pin a length of ribbon to each side of the center panel so that it covers the seamline. Topstitch along both edges of each ribbon.

4 Pin one tassel at each corner on the right side of the pillow back, with the cords running out of the seam allowance and the tassels facing inward. With right sides together, pin the pillow front and back together so that the tassels are sandwiched in between. Machine stitch around all four sides. Machine zigzag stitch the raw edges. Turn the pillow cover right side out and press. Insert the pillow form and close the zipper.

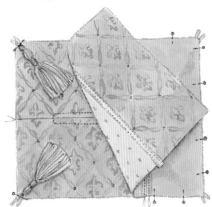

Complement with...

Silk panel pillow
with braiding
Braid gives this softly colored pillow a flamboyant finishing touch. Real silk may need to be dry cleaned, so if the pillow is likely to need regular laundering, use a washable alternative.

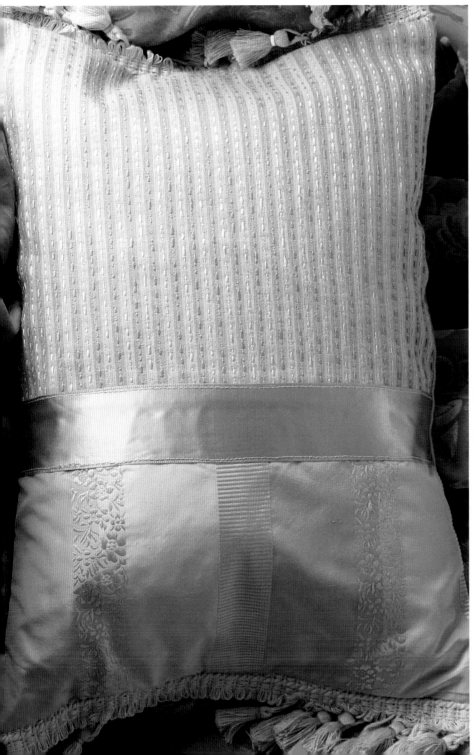

You Will Need
- ½ yd. (0.5 m) of 54-in. (136-cm)-wide home decorating fabric
- 8 x 13¼-in. (20 x 33-cm) piece of silk fabric for the front panel
- 14 in. (36 cm) length of 1½-in. (4-cm)-wide ribbon
- ¾ yd. (70 cm) of 1-in. (2.5-cm)-wide fringed braid
- 10-in. (25-cm) zipper
- 12 x 16-in. (30 x 40-cm) pillow form
- matching polycotton thread

Note: The pillow measures 12 x 16 in. (30 x 40 cm).

Cutting Out
Note: Seam allowances of ⅝ in. (1.5 cm) are included throughout unless otherwise stated.

Cut one 10½ x 13¼-in. (26 x 33-cm) rectangle for the pillow front and two 17¼ x 7¼-in. (43 x 18-cm) rectangles for the pillow back.

 3 HOURS OR LESS

 LOW-SEW PROJECT

The use of these harmonious tones brings all the different elements of the pillow together.

1 Follow Steps 1 and 2 of the Tasseled Pillow with Silk Center Panel, on page 91. With right sides together, pin the front panel to the pillow front piece along one long edge and machine stitch. Press the seam open. Pin the length of ribbon in the center of the right side over the seam and topstitch in place, stitching close to both edges.

2 Pin the fringed braid along both short edges of the pillow front, with the fringe facing inward and the top edge along the seamline. With right sides together, pin the front to the back and stitch along all four sides. Machine zigzag stitch the seams, turn the pillow cover right side out, and press. Insert the pillow form and close the zipper.

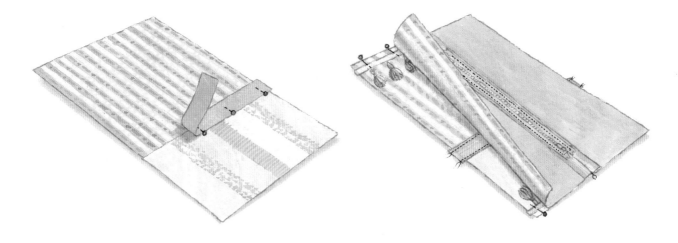

Professional's Tip: Making a Tassel

■ Cut a piece of cardboard the length you want the tassel to be. Wind embroidery floss around it, leaving a loose end at the top. When the tassel is the desired thickness, tie the floss in a knot at the top. Cut across the threads at the base and remove the cardboard.

■ Wrap embroidery floss around the tassel one-eighth and one-quarter of the way down. Knot to secure.

■ In addition to embroidery floss, you can also use thick woolen thread, fine upholstery cord, and even suede or leather thong cord for a modern look.

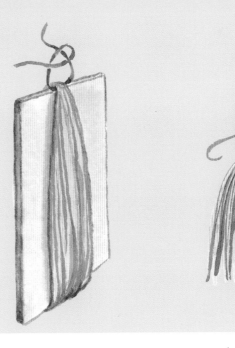

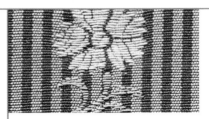

Chunky-edged pillow

Piping, fringing, and braid define the edges of beautiful pillows. Home furnishing stores recognize the importance of these finishing touches and are increasingly stocking bigger and better selections of trim styles and colors. Here, a chunky braid makes a bold color statement and adds a contrasting texture to the piece. Match the trim to a color in the fabric to give a simple pillow a luxurious look. You will need to use a zipper foot on your machine in order to stitch close to the braid.

You Will Need

- ½ yd. (0.5 m) of 54-in. (136-cm)-wide home decorating fabric
- 2 yd. (1.8 m) braid
- 12-in. (30-cm) zipper
- 16-in. (40-cm)-square pillow form
- matching polycotton thread

Note: The pillow measures 16 in. (40 cm) square.

Cutting Out

Note: Seam allowances of ⅝ in. (1.5 cm) are included throughout unless otherwise stated.

Cut one 17¼-in. (43-cm) square for the pillow front, and one 17¼ x 14½-in. (43 x 36-cm) rectangle and one 17¼ x 4-in. (43 x 10-cm) rectangle for the pillow back.

 3 HOURS OR LESS

 SEW PROJECT

The soft edging on this pillow makes it look even more inviting and cozy.

1 With right sides together, pin the large and small pillow back rectangles together along one long edge. Mark 2⅜ in. (6.5 cm) in from each end with pins, then machine stitch from each end up to the marker pins. Now machine baste the center 12 in. (30 cm). Press the seam open.

2 Pin the zipper into the basted part of the seam and baste it in place by hand. Using a zipper foot on the machine, stitch the zipper in place from the right side (see pages 150–151). Remove the hand and machine basting. Open the zipper.

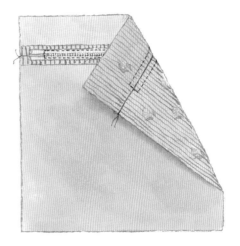

3 Pin the braid to the right side of the pillow front inside the seamline, with the braid facing inward. Gather the braid slightly at the corners so that there will be enough fullness when the cover is turned right side out, and overlap the ends of the braid by ⅜ in. (1 cm). Cut off any excess. Baste the braid in place by hand.

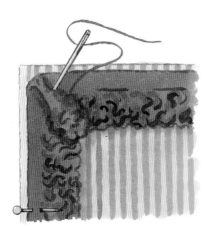

4 With right sides together, pin the pillow front and back together along all four sides, with the braid sandwiched in between. Using a zipper foot and stitching as close to the braid as possible, machine stitch the seam along all sides.

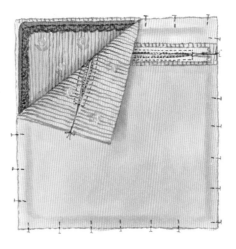

5 Machine zigzag stitch around the edges. Remove the basting and turn the pillow cover right side out. Insert the pillow form and close the zipper.

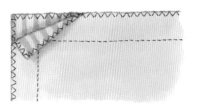

Complement with...

Pillow with ruched piping

In this pillow, fabric is gathered over the piping to create a ruched effect. Cut bias strips from a light- to medium-weight cotton fabric or use a lighter-weight fabric with a different texture, such as taffeta. Make the pillow cover in the same way as the Chunky-Edged Pillow on pages 94–95, following the instructions opposite when you reach Step 3.

You Will Need
- ½ yd. (0.5 m) of 54-in. (136-cm)-wide home decorating fabric
- 2 yd. (1.8 m) of piping cord ¼ in. (6-mm)-thick
- 2-in.(5-cm)-wide strips of piping fabric
- 12-in. (30-cm) zipper
- 16-in. (40-cm) pillow form
- matching polycotton thread

Note: The pillow measures 16 in. (40 cm) square.

Cutting Out
Note: Seam allowances of ⅝ in. (1.5 cm) are included throughout unless otherwise sttated.

Cut the pillow front and back pieces as for the Chunky-Edged Pillow (see page 94).

Cut 2-in. (5-cm)-wide bias strips from the piping fabric as shown on page 154, joining the strips to make a continuous piece 65 in. (165 cm) long.

Cut a length of piping cord long enough to go all around the pillow cover plus 2 in. (5 cm).

 3 HOURS OR LESS

 LOW-SEW PROJECT

The ruched piping on this pillow mirrors the rope pattern in the fabric.

1 Once you have completed the ruched piping following the instructions below, attach it to the pillow by first pinning the piping to the right side of the piece along the edge, with raw edges facing outward and the piping cord inside, following the seamline. Baste in place.

2 Where the two ends of the cord meet, turn under ⅜ in. (1 cm) on the top fabric strip and overlap the fabric strip underneath. Stitch the remainder of the piping in place. Now complete the pillow as on page 95, Steps 4 and 5.

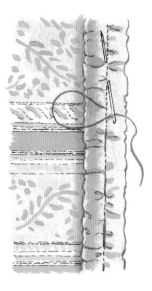

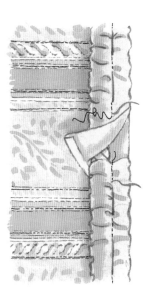

Professional's Tip: Making Ruched Piping

■ Fold the fabric strip in half lengthwise around the piping cord and secure at one end so that the cord is attached.
■ Using a piping foot, stitch ⅝ in. (1.5 cm) from the raw edge for approximately 8 in. (20 cm).
■ With the needle in the fabric, raise the foot on the sewing machine and gently pull the cord through the channel to gather the piping to a length of approximately 4 in. (10 cm).
■ Continue stitching and gathering the piping in short sections until the piping cord meets the end of the bias strip.

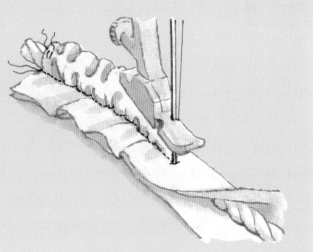

Buttoned circular pillow

This comfortable circular pillow looks equally good among other shapes or on its own on the seat of an upholstered occasional chair. The buttoned center pulls the cover in to give an attractive, plumped-up effect. Remove the buttons before laundering; alternatively, dry clean the pillow.

You Will Need

- ¾ yd. (0.7 m) of 54-in. (136-cm)-wide home decorating fabric
- ½ yd. (0.5 m) of 54-in. (136-cm)-wide contrasting fabric for the piping and covered buttons plus 3½ yd. (3 m) piping cord or 3½ yd. (3 m) ready-made piping
- 14-in. (36-cm) zipper
- two 1½-in. (38-mm) buttons to cover
- 18-in. (45-cm) circular pillow form with 2-in. (5-cm)-deep sides
- matching sewing thread

Note: The pillow measures 18 in. (45 cm) in diameter.

Cutting Out

Note: Seam allowances of ⅝ in. (1.5 cm) are included throughout unless otherwise stated.

From the main fabric, cut two circles 19¼ in. (48 cm) in diameter for the pillow front and back and two 31 x 3¼-in. (80 x 8-cm) rectangles for the side gusset.

If you are making your own piping, prepare 3½ yd. (3 m)—see pages 155–156.

1 Pin the piping around the right side edges of both circles, with the raw edges facing outward and the piped edges inside the seamline. Cut notches in the piping to ease it around the curves, and join the ends of the piping together (see page 155). Baste in place. Right sides together, machine stitch the two gusset strips together along one short edge and press open the seam.

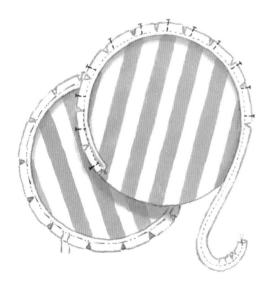

3 HOURS OR LESS

SEW PROJECT

Fabric choice is very important. Here, the contrast between the stripes and the circular shape is very striking.

2 Machine stitch down both long edges of the gusset strip ⅜ in. (1 cm) in from the edges. Right sides together, pin one long edge of the gusset strip around the edge of one of the circles, clipping the seam allowance of the gusset up to the stitching so it will follow the curve.

3 At the point where the short ends of the gusset meet, and allowing a ⅝-in. (1.5-cm) seam allowance on each end, cut off any excess fabric.

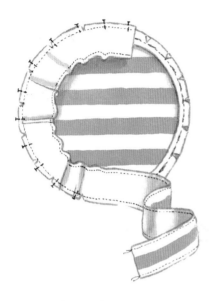

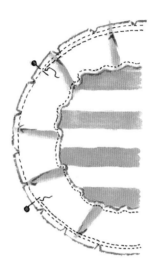

4 Measure 14 in. (36 cm) along the seamline and mark with pins to leave an opening for the zipper. Machine stitch along the seamline. Now machine baste it between the pins. Press open the seam.

5 Pin and hand baste the zipper into the basted part of the seam. Using a zipper foot on the machine, stitch it in place from the right side (see pages 150–151). Remove the hand and machine basting. Open the zipper. Right sides together, machine stitch the short ends of the gusset strip together.

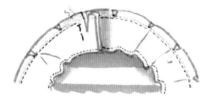

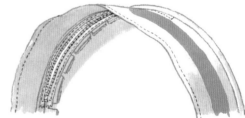

6 Right sides together, pin the other long edge of the gusset to the other circle, clipping up to the stitching line to follow the curve. Machine stitch the pieces together. Finish the raw edges with a machine zigzag stitch and turn the pillow cover right side out.

7 Place the pillow form inside the cover and close the zipper. Make two covered buttons to match the piping fabric (see page 153). Using extra-strong thread and a long needle, stitch them through the center of both sides of the pillow, pulling tightly so that the pillow is nice and plump. Tie a knot securely to fasten.

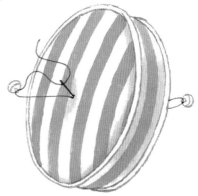

Professional's Tip: Tufting

The kind of buttoned effect shown here—also known as tufting—is the perfect embellishment to a box-style pillow with corded edges.

■ When covering the buttons, first dampen the fabric slightly (a spray bottle will do this efficiently); as it dries, it will shrink to fit the button smoothly.

■ To make sure the buttons are exactly centered, mark each circular piece, before assembling the cover, by folding the piece in half, then in half again, and working a couple of small temporary stitches at the crossing point.

■ Use extra-strong button or carpet thread and a long needle, such as a darner or milliner's needle, to join the two buttons.

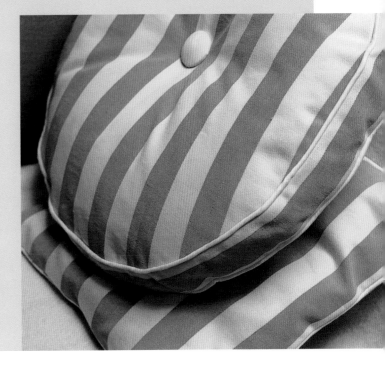

Fringed pillow with appliquéd panel

Fringed with lush cotton and a stylish panel appliquéd to the center, this classic pillow is extremely versatile. The light, fresh-looking colors harmonize well with any decor. Only a small amount of fabric is required for the center panel, which means you can transform a remnant or make a tiny piece of expensive fabric go a long way.

You Will Need

- ⅝ yd. (0.5 m) of 54-in. (136-cm)-wide home decorating fabric
- ¼ yd. (0.3 m) of 54-in. (136-cm)-wide fabric for the center panels
- 2¼ yd. (2 m) of fringed braid
- 14-in. (36-cm) zipper
- 18-in. (45-cm) square pillow form
- matching polycotton thread

Note: The pillow measures 18 in. (45 cm) square.

Cutting Out

Note: Seam allowances of ⅝ in. (1.5 cm) are included throughout unless otherwise stated.

Cut two 19¼-in. (48-cm) squares from the main fabric for the pillow back and front and two 9-in. (23-cm) squares from the second fabric for the center panels.

⏱ **3 HOURS OR LESS**

✂ **LOW-SEW PROJECT**

This pillow combines stripes and checks in soft hues for a graphic effect.

1 Turn under ⅝ in. (1.5 cm) on all sides of the two center panels, trimming and mitering the corners (see page 150) to keep them as flat as possible; baste by hand. With right sides facing up, pin one panel to the center of the pillow front and the other one to the center of the pillow back. Topstitch close to the edges of the center panels.

2 Pin the fringed braid to the right side of one of the pillow pieces, with the fringe facing inward. Gather the fringe slightly at the corners so that it will turn the corners neatly when the pillow cover is turned right side out. Baste the fringe in place by hand.

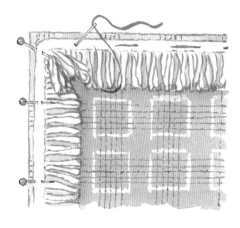

3 With right sides together, pin both pillow pieces together along one edge and machine stitch 2⅜ in. (6 cm) in from each end. Now baste the center 14 in. (36 cm). Press open the seam.

4 Pin the zipper into the basted part of the seam and baste it in place by hand (see pages 150–151). Using a zipper foot on the machine, stitch it in place from the right side. Remove the basting. Open the zipper. With right sides together, pin and stitch the remaining sides together. Zigzag or blanket stitch the seam allowances. Turn the cover right side out. Place the pillow form inside the cover and close the zipper.

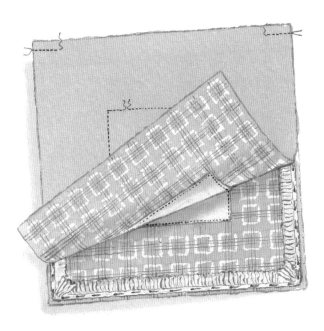

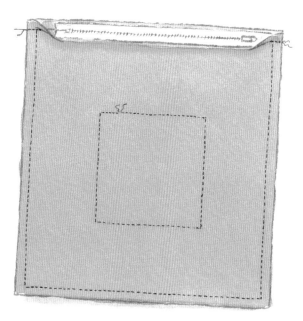

Pillow cover with ties

This leaf-print pillow in spring greens would look wonderful in a sunroom. The contrasting border edging is trimmed with two lines of satin ribbon for a luxurious finish. The design can easily be adapted to fit a rectangular pillow form.

You Will Need

- ⅝ yd. (0.5 m) of 54-in. (136-cm)-wide home decorating fabric
- ⅜ yd. (0.2 m) of 54-in. (136-cm)-wide contrasting fabric
- 1¼ yd. (1 m) of ¼-in. (7-mm)-wide ribbon
- 18-in. (45-cm) square pillow form
- matching polycotton thread

Note: The pillow measures 18 in. (45 cm) square.

Cutting Out

Note: Seam allowances of ⅝ in. (1.5 cm) are included throughout unless otherwise stated.

From the upholstery fabric, cut one 19¼ in. (48 cm) square for the pillow back, one 19¼ x 13¼ in. (48 x 33 cm) rectangle for the pillow front, and one 19¼ x 9½ in. (48 x 24 cm) rectangle for the flap.

From the contrasting fabric, cut one border and one border facing measuring 19¼ x 7¼ in. (48 x 18 cm) and four ties measuring 15 x 3 in. (38 x 8 cm).

1 With right sides together, pin and machine stitch one long edge of the border piece to the right-hand edge of the pillow front. Press the seam toward the border piece.

3 HOURS OR LESS

LOW-SEW PROJECT

This pillow style would suit any boldly patterned fabric.

2 Pin a length of ribbon over the seam on the right side of the pillow front and topstitch close to the ribbon edges. Pin another length of ribbon to the border, 1¼ in. (3 cm) from the first, and topstitch it in the same way.

3 With right sides together, fold one of the ties in half lengthwise. Machine stitch along one short edge and one long edge. Trim the seam. To turn the tie right side out, pin an upholstery needle or clothes pin at the short sewn edge and feed it back through the center of the strip to the open edge. Turn in the open end and slip stitch by hand (see page 149). Make three more ties in the same way and press them.

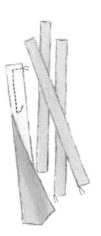

4 Pin two ties to the right side of the front border edge, spacing them equally. Baste in place by hand. Turn under, press, and stitch ⅝ in. (1.5 cm) down one long edge of the border facing. With right sides together, pin the other long edge of the border facing to the front edge of the border, so that the ties are sandwiched in between. Stitch this seam. Turn the border facing to the inside and press. Slip stitch the facing by hand to the back of the stitching that holds the ribbon in place.

5 Turn under ⅜ in. (1 cm) and then ¾ in. (2 cm) along one long edge of the flap and stitch. Pin the remaining two ties to the right side of the pillow back, spacing them evenly. Pin the long, raw edge of the flap to the pillow back, so that the ties are sandwiched in between, and stitch.

6 With right sides together, pin the front of the pillow to the back so that the front border meets the flap edge seam. Fold the flap over to the wrong side of the front and pin. Machine stitch around the remaining three sides. Machine zigzag the seam allowances. Turn the pillow cover right side out and press. Insert the pillow form and tie the ties in bows, as seen below.

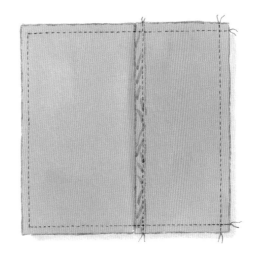

Professional's Tip: Contrast and Variation

The juxtaposition of contrasting fabrics in a project such as this pillow cover can produce an artistic effect. Notice how the solid-colored fabric visually interrupts the main, figured fabric, which then reappears on the underside, just visible at the open edge.

■ Make use of this principle when planning your own original home accessories. For example, if you're planning a patchwork pillow cover using a variety of printed fabrics, you could place a contrasting solid-colored border around the patchwork, then use printed fabric to make the back of the cover.

■ Make fabric ties from two contrasting fabrics. Cut two pieces from each fabric, stitch them together along the two long edges and one short edge, and turn them right side out. This technique could be used for ties on the cover shown here; use either the figured or the solid-colored fabric on the outside.

■ Start a collection of fabrics—some bought and some salvaged from discarded pieces of clothing. You'll find lots of ingenious ways of combining them.

Dining-chair cover with beaded trim

A fitted cover gives a tailored look to a high-backed dining chair. Buttons down the back hold the cover securely in place and make it easy to remove for laundering. For elegance, make a matching set of chair covers; for a fun look, choose different coordinating fabrics for each chair.

You Will Need

- 1½ yd. (1.30 m) of 54-in. (140-cm)-wide upholstery fabric, adding extra for the pattern repeat if necessary
- five 1-in. (2.5-cm) buttons
- 2¼ yd. (2.1 m) beaded trim
- matching polycotton thread

Note: The chair cover fits an upholstered dining chair 38(H) x 21(W) x 20(D) in./96(H) x 52(W) x 50(D) cm. Adjust it to fit your own chair. The skirt is 5½ in. (14 cm) deep, plus trimming.

Cutting Out

Note: Seam allowances of ⅝ in. (1.5 cm) are included throughout unless otherwise stated.

Analyze how the pattern will fall on the fabric when it is on the chair and make sure that pairs of pieces match before you cut them out. Cut one each of pieces 1, 2, and 5, and two each of pieces 3, 4, and 6.

6 TO 8 HOURS

SEW PROJECT

The beaded trim gives this traditional-style floral fabric a contemporary twist.

1 Turn under ⅝ in. (1.5 cm) and then a further
2 in. (5 cm) to the wrong side along the center
back edge of each piece 6 and machine stitch.
Overlap the hemmed edges to close the chair back
and baste along the top edge to hold in place.

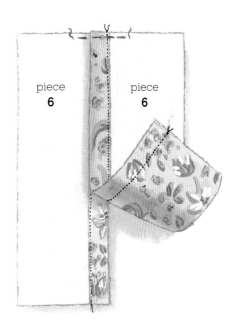

Making the Pattern

Decide how deep the seat skirt will be and mark the hemline on the chair legs using pieces of masking tape. Referring to the diagram on the right, measure the chair and draw the pattern pieces on paper.

For pattern pieces 1, 2, and 3, add a ¾-in. (2-cm) seam allowance all around. The extra ⅛ in. (5 mm) allows for "ease."

For pattern pieces 4 and 5, add a ¾-in. (2-cm) seam allowance to the top and side edges and a 1¼-in. (3-cm) hem allowance to the bottom edge.

For pattern piece 6, add a ¾-in. (2-cm) seam allowance to the top and side edges and a 1¼-in. (3-cm) hem allowance along the bottom edge. Then fold the pattern piece in half lengthwise to find the center of the chair back, and add 3⅝ in. (9 cm) to this side of the pattern. Use this "half piece" when cutting the two pieces 6.

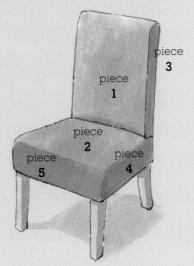

2 With right sides together, pin the top of piece 1 to the basted top edge of the chair back and machine stitch them together, using a ⅝-in. (1.5-cm) seam allowance. With right sides together, pin piece 1 to piece 2. Machine stitch, using a ⅝-in. (1.5-cm) seam allowance, to form the seat and the seat back.

3 Place the assembled cover pieces over the chair with the wrong sides facing outward, and smooth the fabric into the correct position. Pin the side gussets (pieces 3) in place, wrong sides facing out, checking the fit as you do so. Remove the cover from the chair and stitch the side gussets in place, using a ⅝-in. (1.5-cm) seam allowance. Trim the seam to ¼ in. (6 mm) and press.

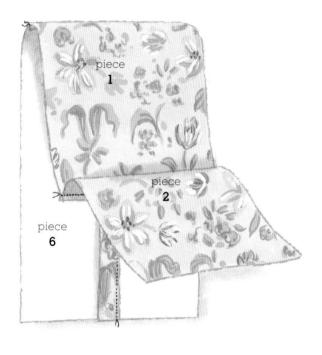

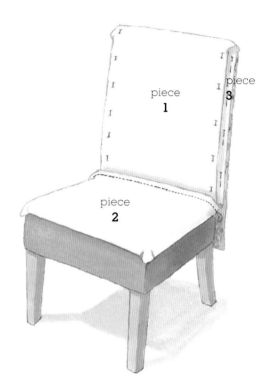

4 Right sides together, pin one piece 4 to each short edge of piece 5. Using a ⅝-in. (1.5-cm) seam allowance, machine stitch each seam, stopping ⅝ in. (1.5 cm) short of the top edge to form the skirt. With right sides together, pin the skirt along one raw gusset edge, the three sides of the seat, and the other gusset edge, matching the skirt seams with the corners. The open seams will allow it to turn the seat corners. Machine stitch, using a ⅝-in. (1.5-cm) seam allowance. Turn to the right side and press the seams flat.

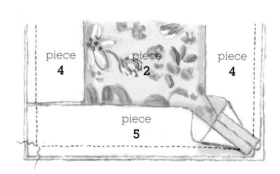

110

5 Place the cover in position on the chair and push the raw side edges of skirt pieces 4 to the wrong sides of the chair back. Pin, then topstitch in place. Remove the cover from the chair and machine zigzag stitch the raw inside edges.

6 Turn under ½ in. (1 cm) followed by ¾ in. (2 cm) along the bottom edge of the chair back and skirt, and pin in place. Machine stitch the hem. Mark the position of the five buttons along the center back hem, spacing them evenly, and work five buttonholes (see pages 151–152). Sew a button in place on the hem underneath to correspond to each buttonhole.

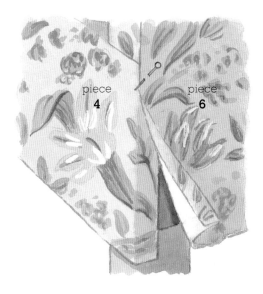

7 Pin the beaded trim along the hemmed edge of the skirt and machine stitch in place, overlapping the ends to complete.

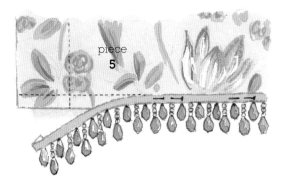

Professional's Tip: Buttonholes

If you'd prefer not to make buttonholes, by hand or machine, you could instead make thread loops (several strands of thread closely covered with buttonhole stitch) along the edge.

■ Alternatively, fasten the edges of the cover with two or more pairs of fabric or ribbon ties (see, for example, page 121).

■ After turning each tie right side out and pressing it, turn in the remaining raw edges at the open end, baste them in place, and topstitch the tie to the cover in a neat square pattern. Allow enough space between each pair of ties for a graceful bow.

Complement with...

Dining-chair cover with pleated back

Another decorative way of fastening the chair cover is to make an inverted pleat down the back, in either the same fabric as the chair cover or a contrasting one. Generous fabric or ribbon ties add an extra flourish. The extra fabric formed by the pleat makes it easy to slip the cover on or off the chair. The pattern layout is the same as for the Cover with Beaded Trim; you simply need to adapt piece 6 slightly.

You Will Need

As for Dining-Chair Cover with Beaded Trim plus:

- a piece of contrasting fabric the length of the chair back x 13 in. (33 cm)
- 2 yd. (1.8 m) of 1½-in. (35-mm)-wide ribbon or 16 x 12 in. (40 x 28 cm) extra fabric to make the ties

Cutting Out

Note: Seam allowances of ⅝ in. (1.5 cm) are included throughout unless otherwise stated.

Look at how the pattern will fall on the chair cover and make sure that pairs of pieces match before you cut them out. Cut one each of pieces 1, 2, 5, and the inverted pleat, and two each of pieces 3, 4, and 6. Cut four 16 x 3-in. (40 x 7-cm) strips of fabric if you are making your own ties.

🕐 3 HOURS OR LESS

🪡 SEW PROJECT

Ribbon ties add a theatrical finish to these stylish covers.

1 Cut the ribbon into four equal lengths or make four ties as follows. With right sides together, fold each strip of fabric in half lengthwise. Pin and machine stitch along one short edge and down the long edge, using ⅝-in. (1.5-cm) seams. Trim the seam to ¼ in. (6 mm), then turn to the right side and press flat. Pin the ties in two pairs, raw edges together, to the right sides of the center back edges (pieces 6) and baste in place. With right sides together, pin the pleat rectangle to both center back edges. Machine stitch the pleat rectangle to the center back edges, using ⅝-in. (1.5-cm) seams.

2 Press the seams. Bring the seams to meet in the center of the chair back. Press the fold along each seamline. Baste the pleat in position along the top edge. Follow Steps 2–6 of the Dining-Chair Cover with Beaded Trim on pages 110–111 to make up the seat cover, omitting the buttonholes and buttons.

Making the Pattern

Draw pattern pieces 1–5 on paper (see page 109.)

For piece 6, measure the chair back and add a ¾-in. (2-cm) seam allowance on the top and side edges and a 1¼-in. (3-cm) hem allowance along the bottom edge. Fold the pattern piece in half lengthwise to find the center back seam, and

add a ⅝-in. (1.5-cm) seam allowance to this edge. Use this "half-piece" when cutting the two pieces 6.

To make a pattern for the inverted pleat, draw a rectangle the same length as the center back and 13 in. (33 cm) wide.

Button-and-tab seat cover

A simple, loose cover, held securely in place by means of tabs with buttonholes or Velcro, instantly brightens up worn upholstery on a pretty country chair. The seat-cover skirt can be flat and tailored, ruffled, or pleated with ribbon ties. The finished cover fits a seat 15½ in. (40 cm) square and the skirt is 3½ in. (9 cm) deep.

You Will Need

- pattern paper and pencil
- ½ yd. (0.5m) of 60-in. (150-cm)-wide linen
- 8 buttons or felt flowers
- 2.5 yd. (2.2 m) of rick-rack braid
- scraps of medium-weight iron-on interfacing
- stick-on Velcro pads (optional)

Cutting Out

Note: Add a ⅝-in. (1.5-cm) seam allowance on all sides for all pattern pieces except the tabs.

Measure the width and depth of the chair seat, allowing for areas that need to be cut away around the bars. Draw on pattern paper.

For the skirt sides, front, and back, draw rectangles 3½ in. (9 cm) deep, plus seam allowances, and the width of the side of the chair seat in length, plus seam allowances.

For the front tab, draw a 5½ x 1½-in. (14 x 3.5-cm) rectangle. For the back tab, draw a 4 x 1½-in. (10.5 x 3.5-cm) rectangle. Place the patterns on the fabric following the grain. Cut:

1 seat piece
2 side skirt pieces
1 front skirt piece
1 back skirt piece
4 front tabs and 4 back tabs

Cut 2 front tab and 2 back tab pieces in interfacing

 3 HOURS OR LESS

 LOW-SEW PROJECT

Bold colors work well with painted furniture.

1 Machine stitch a guide line ⅝ in. (1.5 cm) in from the edges (along the seam allowance) on both back corners of the seat piece where it goes around the back bars. Turn under the seam allowance, snipping the seam allowance at the inside corner where necessary to make hems. Stitch in place.

2 Turn under ¼ in. (5 mm) followed by ⅜ in. (1 cm) along the three outside edges of each skirt piece, mitering the outer corners (see page 150). Machine stitch in place. Sew rick-rack braid along the hemmed edges of each skirt piece.

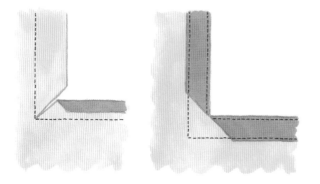

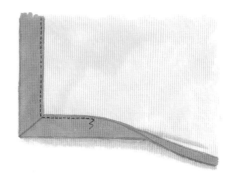

3 With right sides together, pin the front skirt to the front edge of the seat and sew together along the seamline. Trim the seam to ½ in. (1 cm), zigzag stitch, and press. Sew the other three skirt pieces to the seat in the same way.

4 Take two front tab pieces and iron a piece of interfacing to the wrong side of one piece. Right sides together, pin and then stitch them together around the edges, using a ¼-in. (5 mm) seam and leaving an opening of 1¼ in. (3 cm). Turn right side out. Slip stitch the opening closed and press the tab flat. Make the other front tab and the two back tabs in the same way.

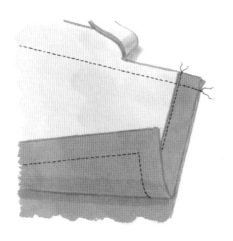

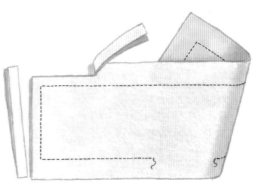

5 Place the seat cover on the chair and pin the tabs in position on the skirt pieces. Sew a decorative button in place on one front tab, stitching through all thicknesses to attach it to the skirt. Stitch a button to the other end of the tab and stick Velcro pads to the underside of the tab and its matching position on the skirt to secure. Fix the other three tabs in place in the same way.

Complement with...

Damask seat cover
In this simple but stylish project, two damask napkins are transformed into a pretty seat cover. The edges of the napkins are already hemmed, which cuts down on the sewing time, and the napkins that we used had a symmetrical pattern, so it is very easy to match up the fabric on the front and side flaps.

You Will Need
- 2 matching damask napkins 16 in. (40 cm) square
- 1¼ yd. (1.2 m) gathered trim
- 3¼ yd. (2.9 m) of ½-in. (12-mm)-wide ribbon
- matching sewing thread

Note: The seat cover fits a chair seat approximately 15 in. (37 cm) square.

Cutting Out
Note: Seam allowances of ⅝ in. (1.5-cm) are included throughout unless otherwise stated.

Cut a 4⅝-in. (11.5-cm) strip from opposite sides of one napkin to make the side flaps. Cut the remaining piece of the napkin to 5¼ in. (13 cm) wide to make the front flap. Leave the other napkin whole, as this will form the seat of the cover.

3 HOURS OR LESS

LOW-SEW PROJECT

Transform napkins into seat covers to create a coordinated look with existing table linen.

1 Turn under a ⅝-in. (1.5-cm) hem on one short edge of each of the side flaps (making this the same edge on both), and machine stitch. Turn under a ⅝-in. (1.5-cm) hem on each short edge and one long edge of the front flap and machine stitch.

2 With right sides together, center the remaining edge of the front flap on one side of the whole napkin, pin, and machine stitch. Press the seam open.

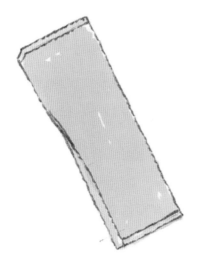

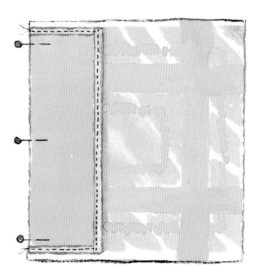

3 With right sides together, pin the side flaps to the sides of the whole napkin, with the hemmed edge of each side flap at the front. Machine stitch, then press the seams open.

4 Pin and machine stitch a length of gathered trimming along the bottom edge of the front and side flaps. Cut eight 14-in. (36-cm) lengths of ribbon. Pin the ribbons in corresponding pairs along the front flap, back edge, and side flaps, referring to the drawing below. Stitch in place.

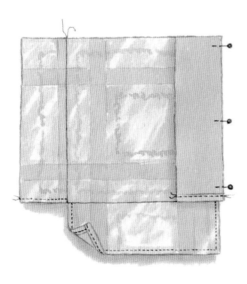

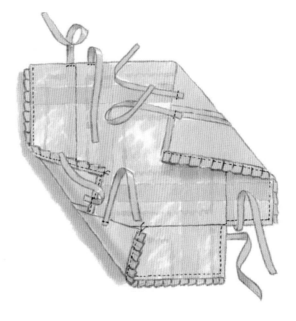

Kitchen-chair pillow

Wooden kitchen chairs are practical, but they do need a bit of padding to make them comfortable. A tailored cover is a smart way to soften the seat and bring style to the kitchen—and by cutting the foam pillow pad to the exact shape of the chair seat, you can get a really precise fit. Blue-and-white is a lovely, fresh-looking color combination that will brighten up even the most jaded kitchen decor, and the sprigs of yellow flowers on this fabric add a hint of early-morning summer sunshine.

You Will Need

- pattern paper
- pencil
- 20-in. (50-cm) square of 1-in. (2.5-cm) thick foam
- 20-in. (50-cm) square of home decorating fabric for the pillow top
- 20-in. (50-cm) square of home decorating fabric for the pillow back
- 12 x 20 in. (30 x 50 cm) piece of fabric for the ties
- Fabric cut on the bias and 2 yd. (1.9 m) piping cord or 2 yd./1.9 m ready-made piping
- 10-in. (25-cm) zipper

Note: The pillow measures 15¾ x 17¾ in. (40 x 45 cm). Adjust the size to fit your own chair.

 3 HOURS OR LESS

 LOW-SEW PROJECT

1 Fold the pattern paper in half and place it on the chair seat, aligning the midpoint of the chair with the fold of the paper. Draw around the edge of the seat. Draw a second line ⅝ in. (1.5 cm) beyond the first, for the seam allowance. Cut out the pattern and open out the pattern paper. Cut one piece of fabric for the pillow top and one for the pillow back. Using a sharp craft knife, cut the foam to the same size as the pattern minus the seam allowance.

A padded foam pillow is a quick way of adding comfort to the kitchen.

2 Make a strip of piping 52 in. (132 cm) long (see page 155). Pin and baste it around the right side of the pillow top, with the raw edge facing outward and the piped edge just inside the seamline. Snip into the piping seam allowance to turn the corners. Join the ends of the piping cord (see page 155).

3 Now make the ties. Cut a strip of fabric measuring 3 x 16½ in. (8 x 42 cm), following the grain of the fabric. Fold the strip in half lengthwise, right sides together. Using a ½-in. (13-mm) seam, stitch along one short edge and down the long edge. Trim the seam, turn the tie right side out, and press flat, with the seam running down the center of the tie. Make three more ties in the same way.

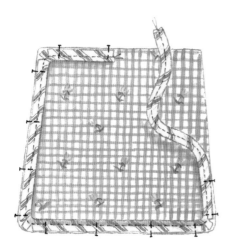

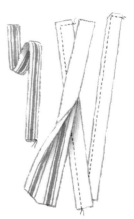

4 With raw edges even, pin and baste a tie to the right side of the back edge of the pillow back, approximately 2 in. (5 cm) in from the side edge. Pin and baste another tie to the back edge, 2 in. (5 cm) in from the opposite side edge.

5 Right sides together, pin the pillow back to the top along the back edge. Mark the center 10 in. (25 cm) along the back edge with pins. Machine stitch up to the pins from each end. Now machine baste the center 10 in. (25 cm). Press open the seam. Pin and hand baste the zipper into the basted part of the seam (see pages 150–151). Using a zipper foot, stitch the zipper in place from the right side. Remove the hand and machine basting. Open the zipper.

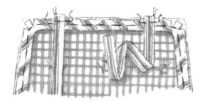

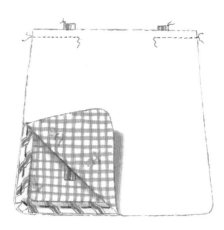

6 Pin and baste the remaining two ties along the side edges of the pillow back, approximately 1 in. (2.5 cm) down from the back edge. Right sides together, pin the front of the pillow to the back and machine stitch along the three remaining sides, stitching as close as possible to the stitching line of the piping. Turn the pillow cover right side out and remove any basting stitches. Insert the foam pad and close the zipper.

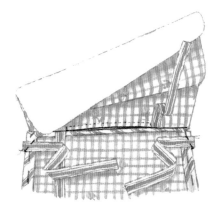

Professional's Tip: Ribbon Ties

Fabric ties can easily be made by the method shown in Step 3, which produces a seam on one edge. A more refined effect is produced if the seam is centered on the underside of the tie.

■ First fold the strip, right sides together, and stitch along the long edge as shown in Step 3, but not along either end. Trim the seam allowances and press them open.

■ Leaving the strip wrong side out, move the seam to the center. Lightly press the strip flat, then stitch across one end. Press and trim the seam, then turn the strip right side out. (A knitting needle will help at the corners.)

■ Press the strip flat.

chapter five

ACCESSORIES

Attention to detail is the hallmark of true style. This final section sets out some quick-and-easy projects for those all-important finishing decorative touches.

Pleated lampshade with beaded trim

Here, a straight-sided shade, known as an Empire shade, has been covered with regular pleats and trimmed at the base with attractive beading. Use lightweight cotton fabric or silk to prevent the shade from becoming too bulky.

You Will Need

- straight-sided lampshade frame 6¼ in. (15.5 cm) high
- ½ yd. (40 cm) of 45-in. (115-cm)-wide lightweight cotton or silk fabric
- 2¼ yd. (2 m) of ½-in. (1-cm) binding tape
- fabric glue
- ¾ yd. (70 cm) beaded trim
- matching sewing thread

Note: The lampshade has a top ring 4 in. (10 cm) in diameter and a bottom ring 8 in. (20 cm) in diameter. Adjust the fabric amounts to fit your own shade.

Cutting Out

Cut two 23 x 7¼-in. (58 x 19-cm) rectangles of fabric for the front and back panels. Each fabric panel will be pleated to cover half the shade, with end pleats overlapping by ½ in. (1 cm).

Cut bias strips 1¼ in. (3 cm) wide, joining them together to make a continuous 41-in. (102-cm) length to fit around the circumference of the top and bottom rings. Fold in and press the raw edges by ¼ in. (5 mm).

 3 HOURS OR LESS

 LOW-SEW PROJECT

A colored fabric shade will give the same color glow.

1 Wind binding tape around the top and bottom rings of the frame.

2 Make 22 evenly spaced pleats along the top edge of one panel of fabric, holding the pleats in place with pins. Pleat the second panel in the same way.

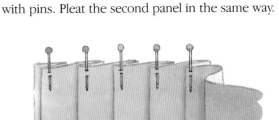

3 With the fabric overlapping the frame, pin the first panel along the top edge of the frame, pinning the fabric to the binding tape. Pull the pleats down to the bottom ring, keeping the pleat edges on the straight of the fabric, and fan them out evenly to fit the frame, pinning as you go. Pin the other piece to the frame in the same way, overlapping the end pleats to hide the joins.

4 Hem stitch (see page 149) the top and bottom pleats in place around the frame, stitching them to the binding tape, and trim off the excess fabric.

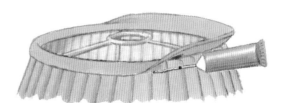

5 With the right side of the bias binding to the inside of the frame top, slip stitch one folded edge in place, folding over and overlapping the ends where they meet. Fold the binding over to the right side of the shade and glue it in place. Repeat at the base of the frame. Pin the beaded trimming around the inside of the lampshade base and slip stitch it in place.

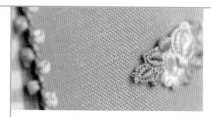

Complement with...

No-sew lampshade *This no-sew*
lampshade is a great way of using up fabric scraps to create
a really special piece. For the best results, choose a shade
with a simple basic shape and straight sloping sides.

You Will Need
- medium-sized, fabric-covered lampshade with 8 panels
- clothes brush (optional)
- pattern paper and pencil
- ½ yd. (45 cm) solid blue cotton fabric
- ½ yd. (45 cm) cotton gingham fabric
- clothespins
- fabric glue or spray adhesive
- 1½ yd. (1.3 m) rick-rack braid for trimming
- 1¼ yd. (1.4 m) of ¼-in. (5-mm)-wide blue velvet ribbon
- 4 floral silk motifs

3 HOURS OR LESS

NO-SEW PROJECT

Note: Be sure to use the spray adhesive in a well-ventilated area.

Mix plains and patterns for a stylish look that could coordinate with other soft furnishings.

1 If you use an old lampshade, brush it down with a clothes brush to remove any dust. Measure around the shade to find the circumference at both top and bottom, mark eight evenly spaced points on both the top and bottom, and make a paper pattern for the panels. You do not need to add a seam allowance when cutting this pattern.

2 Pin the shade panel pattern on the blue fabric and cut out four panels. Repeat on the gingham fabric, cutting out four panels.

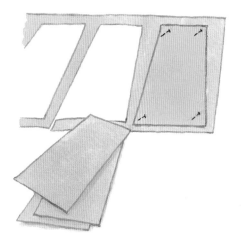

3 Using clothespins, position the eight panels around the lampshade without overlapping them, alternating the blue and gingham fabrics. Using fabric glue or spray adhesive, glue the panels to the lampshade, and readjust the clothespins to keep the fabric taut. Cut eight equal lengths of rick-rack braid ½ in. (1 cm) shorter than the depth of the lampshade.

4 Using spray adhesive, glue the rick-rack in place to cover the joins between the panels. Cut the velvet ribbon to fit the top and bottom circumferences of the shade, and glue them in place, making sure you tuck the ribbon ends in neatly with a dab of glue. Finally, glue the floral trimmings to each of the blue panels with a dab of spray adhesive. Allow to dry for 24 hours.

Fabric-covered photo frame

Covering a frame with fabric gives a lovely, soft look to family photographs. It is also ideal for inclusion in a group of pictures, adding color, pattern, and textural interest to the display. A plush layer of interlining gently plumps up the surface to give a padded effect. Choose a frame that has a flat face and simple lines, so that the fabric will mold itself to the shape. Adjust the measurements to suit your own frame.

You Will Need

- 13½ x 11-in. (34.5 x 31-cm) piece of cotton fabric
- 8½ x 7-in. (21.5 x 18-cm) piece of batting or curtain interlining
- picture frame, 8½ x 7 x ⅝ in. (21.5 x 18 x 1.5 cm)
- fabric stiffening spray
- spray adhesive
- high-tack craft adhesive
- 17-in. (43-cm) length of ⅜-in. (1-cm)-wide ribbon

 3 HOURS OR LESS

 NO-SEW PROJECT

Note: Be sure to use the spray adhesive in a well-ventilated area.

This no-sew project would make a very personal gift for family and friends.

1 Spray the wrong side of the cotton fabric with stiffening spray and leave until it is completely dry. Cut a piece of batting or interlining the same size as the front of the frame. Measure the aperture of the frame and cut a hole this size in the center of the batting or interlining. Spray adhesive to the back of the batting and stick it to the front of the frame.

2 Measure the height and width of the front of the frame. Add the depth of the frame on all four sides, plus the depth of the recess around the aperture, plus the width of the frame back. Cut a rectangle of stiffened fabric to these measurements. Using a soft pencil or tailor's chalk, draw a rectangle the size of the aperture in the center of the wrong side of the fabric. Measure the depth of the aperture recess, mark this distance inside the first rectangle, and draw a second rectangle along those marks. Cut out the smaller rectangle, and snip the fabric at each corner up to the corner of the larger drawn rectangle.

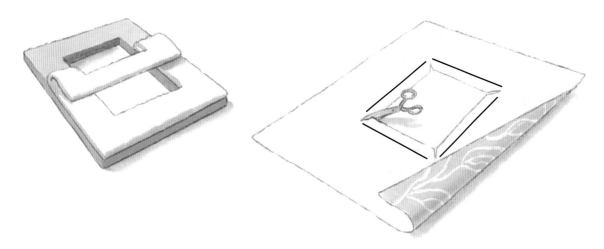

3 Spray the back of the fabric with adhesive and place the frame on top, batting side down. Cut the sides of the fabric level with the frame corners, leaving a square tab the depth of the frame uncut at each corner. At the top and bottom of the frame, cut the fabric level with the frame corners. Fold the sides over the back and secure with high-tack adhesive. Repeat with the top and bottom flaps, and fold in the square corner tabs, again securing with adhesive.

4 Apply craft adhesive to the fabric edges on the inside of the aperture and stick them down, smoothing out any wrinkles. Cut a length of ribbon to fit all around the inside of the aperture so that the ends overlap, and glue the ribbon in position to cover the edges of the fabric.

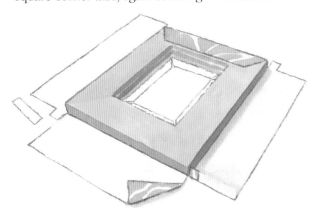

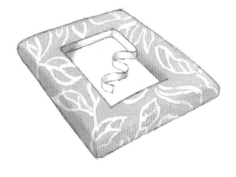

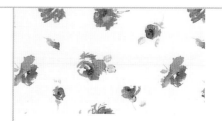

Shadow box frame

We all have cherished mementos and collections of objects that we've gathered over the years. It's lovely to display them for all to see, rather than tuck them away in a drawer or closet. Baby's first bootees, for example, make a charming decoration for a nursery. A box frame is a chic way of displaying them. Commercial plain wooden box frames can be bought from frame and craft stores. Cover and line them with pretty fabrics to match your room's color scheme and use double-sided self-adhesive pads or craft adhesive to hold the objects securely in place.

You Will Need

- 15 x 16½-in. (38 x 42-cm) piece of cotton lawn fabric for the outside
- 27 x 9½-in. (68 x 24-cm) piece of fabric to line the box
- fabric stiffening spray
- spray adhesive
- high-tack craft adhesive
- masking tape
- scrap paper
- commercial box frame

Note: The frame measures 9¼ x 7¼ x 2¾ in. (23.5 x 18.5 x 7 cm). Adapt to fit your own box frame.

 3 HOURS OR LESS

NO-SEW PROJECT

Note: Be sure to use the spray adhesive in a well-ventilated area.

Use a plain or less detailed fabric to line the box so that the objects are displayed clearly.

1 Spray the wrong side of both fabrics with stiffening spray and leave until completely dry. Remove the back of the box frame and cut a piece of lining fabric to the same size, adding ⅝ in. (1.5 cm) all around. Spray adhesive on the right side of the frame back and smooth the fabric over the wood, folding the edges over and securing with craft adhesive.

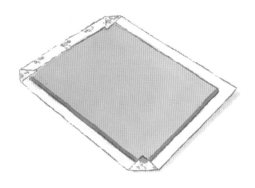

2 Cut a strip of lining fabric the depth of the inside of the box and the combined length of all four sides plus an overlap of ½ in. (1 cm). Mask the glass inside and out, using masking tape and scrap paper. Spray adhesive onto the inside of the box and stick the fabric strip in place, overlapping the ends.

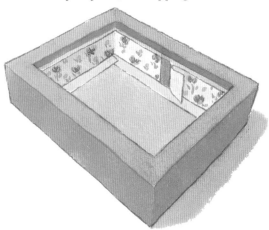

3 Measure the depth of the box plus the front of the frame, the recess, and the back of the frame. Cut a strip from the cotton lawn fabric to this width and long enough to fit all around the four sides of the box plus a ½ in. (1 cm) overlap. Apply spray adhesive to the box. Lay the fabric strip on a flat surface with the wrong side facing you, and place the box in the center of the strip. Smooth the fabric around the box, securing the ends with adhesive.

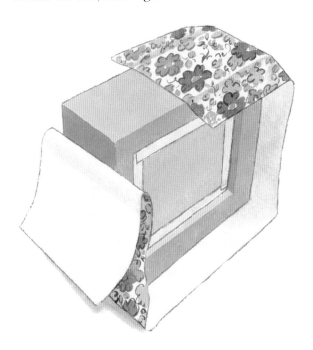

4 Spray adhesive over the front of the frame. Fold in the fabric at each corner to make a neat miter and glue in place. Apply adhesive to the edges of the fabric and push them down neatly into the recess. Fold in the corners on the frame back in the same way and glue in place. Remove the masking tape and scrap paper. To fix the shoes in place, coat both soles with craft adhesive, and press firmly to the back of the frame, pressing down inside the shoes.

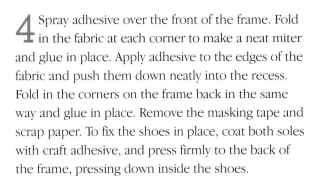
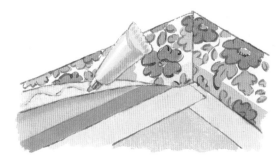

Box file

Box files help to keep desktops clutter-free. Buying smart, decorative box files ready made can be expensive, so making your own is the practical solution. Made from layers of mountboard glued together and covered with pretty fabrics, they look great stacked side by side on shelves. Make a matching set—or use a different fabric or pattern for each category to make them easy to identify. You might, for example, choose a different color for your accounts, your favorite recipes collected from magazines, or a bundle of precious love letters.

You Will Need

- ¾ yd. (0.7 m) of 54-in. (137-cm)-wide cotton fabric
- Two 23⅜ x 33-in. (59.5 x 84-cm) sheets of stiff craft board
- spray adhesive
- fabric stiffening spray
- high-tack craft adhesive
- 36-in. (90-cm) length of 2-in. (5-cm)-wide self-adhesive linen tape
- 3-in. (8-cm) length of ⅜-in. (1-cm)-wide ribbon
- craft knife
- steel ruler
- cutting mat
- clear cellophane tape

Note: The box file measures 9¾ x 13 x 3 in. (25 x 33 x 8 cm).

⏱ **6 TO 8 HOURS**

NO-SEW PROJECT

Note: Be sure to use the spray adhesive in a well-ventilated area.

A ribbon tie gives a box file a feminine finishing touch.

1 Place the ironed fabric on a flat surface, spray the back with fabric stiffening spray, and leave until it is completely dry. Apply glue to the ends of one piece 1 and stick the number 2 pieces to it. Secure with small pieces of cellophane tape. Attach the remaining piece 1 in the same way to form a frame.

2 Cut a piece of fabric measuring 44 x 4 in. (113 x 10 cm). Apply spray adhesive to the outside of the frame and stick the fabric to it, covering all four sides and overlapping the ends, leaving an even border top and bottom. Fold the excess fabric over to the inside along the top and bottom, securing in place along each edge with craft adhesive.

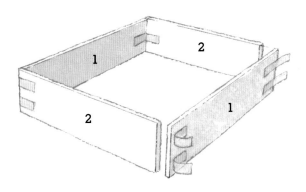

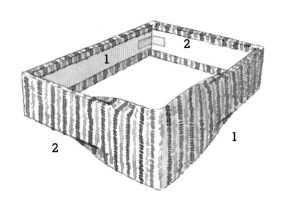

Cutting Out

■ Using a craft knife and steel ruler on a cutting mat, measure and cut out the following from stiff craft board:

■ Six pieces measuring 12¼ x 3 in. (31 x 7 cm). Glue together in threes to form two panels (pieces 1).

■ Six pieces measuring 9½ x 3 in. (24 x 7 cm). Glue together in threes to form two panels (pieces 2).

■ Two pieces measuring 13 x 10 in. (33 x 25 cm). Glue them together to form one panel (piece 3).

■ Three pieces measuring 13 x 3 in. (33 x 7 cm). Glue together to form one panel (piece 4).

■ Two pieces measuring 13 x 9½ in. (33 x 24 cm). Glue together to form one panel (piece 5).

■ Four pieces measuring 9½ x 1 in. (24 x 2.5 cm). Glue together in pairs to form two panels (pieces 6).

■ Two pieces measuring 13 x 1 in. (33 x 2.5 cm). Glue together to form one piece (piece 7).

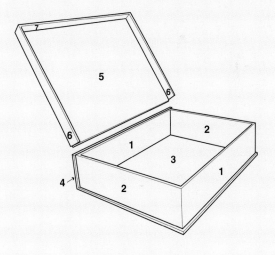

3 Apply craft adhesive to the bottom edge of piece 4 and stick it along the back edge of piece 3, securing with adhesive tape on both sides.

4 To make the lid, apply craft adhesive along the bottom edge of piece 7 and stick it along the back edge of piece 5. Stick pieces 6 along the short edges of piece 5, securing all joins with tape. Cut a 17-in. (43-cm) length of linen tape. As seen below, join piece 4 to piece 5 with the linen tape (as below), leaving ¼ in. (5 mm) of tape between the two pieces of craft board. Snip the tape level with the edge of the lid so that the ends can be folded neatly over the corners of the lid and piece 4.

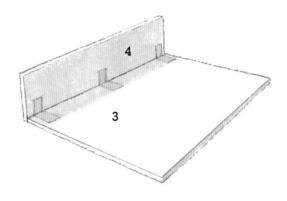

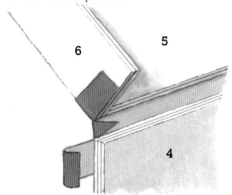

5 Cut a piece of fabric measuring 13½ x 14½ in. (34 x 37 cm). Spray the underside of piece 3 and the back of piece 4 with adhesive, and stick the fabric in place so that the long edge of the fabric aligns with the long edge of piece 4 and extends by equal amounts beyond the pieces on all other sides.

6 Where the fabric extends beyond the edge of the base, cut off an end piece to leave an overhang of approximately ⅜ in (1 cm) at each corner, ensuring the inner edge extends just under the base. Fold up the overhanging piece around the corner to create a neat edge and stick in place. Fold up the remaining sides and stick in place.

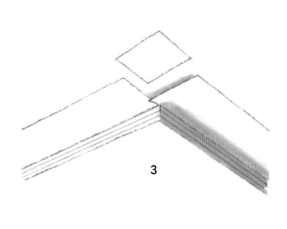

7 Stick a length of linen tape measuring 12½ in. (32 cm) along the inside join of piece 4 and the lid to match the position of the tape on the outside.

8 Stick the frame shape onto the base and back with craft adhesive, securing with tape on the inside. Cut a piece of fabric measuring 11 x 17½ in. (28 x 45 cm). Spray the top and sides of the outside of the lid with adhesive and stick on the fabric, making sure the cut edge forms a neat and even line, overlapping the tape edge. Snip the two front corners from the front edge of the fabric to the corners of the lid and glue the flap over the lip to the inside of the lid. Fold over the remaining flap of fabric and stick it in place to create neat corners.

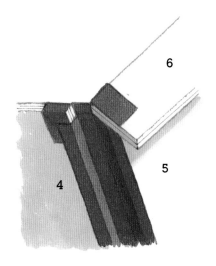

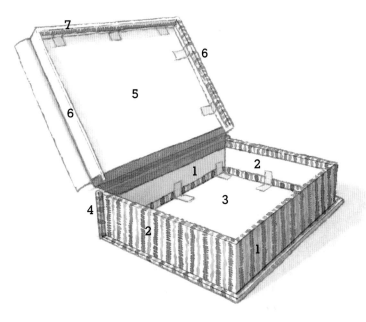

9 Fold the length of ribbon in half and glue it to the inside of the lid, in the center, to form a loop. Cut a length of fabric measuring 43½ x 2¾ in. (110 x 6.5 cm). Spray the back of the fabric with adhesive and stick it around the sides of the inside of the box, ¼ in. (5 mm) down from the top edge.

10 Cut a rectangle of fabric measuring 12¼ x 9 in. (31 x 23 cm) and glue it to the base of the inside of the box. Cut a rectangle of fabric measuring 13 x 9½ in. (32.5 x 24 cm) and glue it to the inside of the lid.

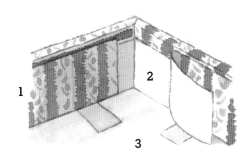

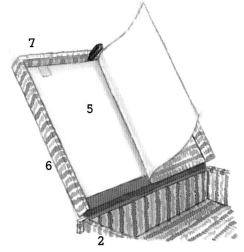

Complement with...

No-sew home office folder

To match your box files, make a range of desk accessories, such as this stylish folder. Use a small-scale printed cotton fabric and pick out one of the print colors for the solid-colored spine and ties. The self-adhesive linen tape used for the spine is available from bookbinding material suppliers.

You Will Need

- ½ yd. (0.5 m) 54-in. (137-cm)-wide cotton fabric
- cardboard
- 26 in. (66 cm) length of 2-in. (5-cm)-wide self-adhesive linen tape
- fabric stiffening spray
- spray adhesive
- high-tack craft adhesive
- 24-in. (60-cm) length of ⅜-in. (1-cm)-wide ribbon
- craft knife
- steel ruler
- cutting mat

Note: The folder measures 10 x 12½ in. (25 x 31.5 cm).

Cutting Out

Using a craft knife and steel ruler on a cutting mat, cut four 10 x 12½-in. (25 x 31.5-cm) rectangles of cardboard. Using spray adhesive, glue them together in pairs to make the folder front and back.

Spray the wrong side of the fabric with stiffening spray and leave until it is completely dry. Following the grain of the fabric, cut two 10⅝ x 14½-in. (27 x 37-cm) rectangles for the front and back and two 10¼ x 13-in. (26 x 33-cm) rectangles for the lining.

Note: Be sure to use the spray adhesive in a well-ventilated area.

 3 HOURS OR LESS

 NO-SEW PROJECT

A striped fabric suits the angular nature of desk accessories.

1 Place the cardboard folder front and back side by side, with a ½-in. (1-cm) gap between them. Peel the backing from the linen tape and stick the center section of the tape over the gap so that it overlaps the cardboard inside edges by ¾ in. (2 cm). Turn the cardboard pieces over. Fold the tape over at the top and bottom edges so that the ends meet in the middle. This will be the inside of the folder.

2 Apply spray adhesive to the wrong side of the front fabric piece. Stick it to the outside of the front of the folder, so that the fabric overlaps the linen tape by ⅜ in. (1 cm). Working from the center outward, smooth out the fabric with your hands to get rid of any air bubbles.

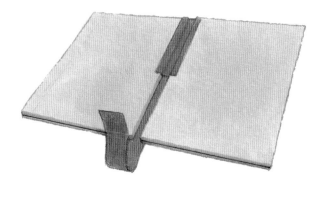

3 Stick fabric to the back of the folder in the same way. Turn the folder over so that the inside is facing you. Fold over and stick down the fabric that extends beyond the cardboard, mitering the corners to create a neat finish (see page 150).

4 Cut the ribbon into two equal lengths. Find the center point of the two front edges on the inside of the folder. Glue one end of each ribbon to these points 1 in. (2.5 cm) in from the edge. Fold under and press ⅝ in. (1.5 cm) to the wrong side on all four edges on both lining pieces. Spray adhesive to the wrong side of both lining pieces and apply high-tack adhesive along the edges. Stick them in place, aligning the long edges with the fabric folded over from the front of the folder.

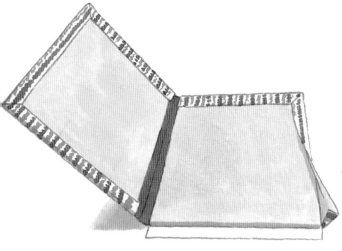

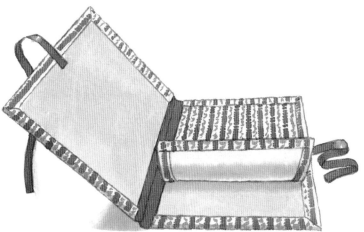

Padded headboard

A headboard provides elegant decoration for your bedroom—and no sewing skills are required. This headboard is padded with a layer of batting and covered in a striking, striped fabric. Wooden studs hold the board level with the top edge of the mattress. You may need to adjust the length of the studs to fit your own bed.

1 Draw a horizontal line across the MDF 14 in. (36 cm) up from the bottom edge. Mark the center point of this line, then measure and mark 9 in. (23 cm) out from the center mark in each direction.

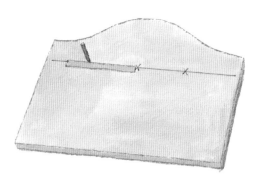

You Will Need

- paper to make a template
- 1¾ yd. (1.5 m) of 55-in. (140-cm)-wide fabric
- 39 x 23½-in. (99 x 60-cm) piece of ½-in. (12-mm)-thick MDF (medium density fiberboard)
- jigsaw, goggles, and mask
- fine-grade sandpaper
- ruler and pencil
- hand drill and bit
- 39 x 23½-in. (99 x 60-cm) piece of 8-oz (250-g) polyester batting
- high-tack craft adhesive
- staple gun and staples suitable for MDF
- bradawl
- 24-in. (60-cm) length of 1-in. (25-mm)-wide grosgrain ribbon
- three 1⅛-in. (3-cm) buttons to cover
- 3 plain buttons
- long needle and thread
- 48-in. (1.2-m) length of 1⅜ x ½-in. (3.5 x 1.5-cm) studs
- 4 wood screws

Note: The finished headboard measures 39 x 23½ in. (99 x 60 cm) and fits a standard single bed.

 6 TO 8 HOURS

 LOW-SEW PROJECT

Cutting Out

Make a template for half of the headboard by drawing the curved shape to size on a piece of paper folded in half so that, when the paper is opened out, the shape is perfectly symmetrical. Copy the shape onto the MDF. Working in a well-ventilated area, wearing goggles and a mask, cut the shaped top of the headboard using a jigsaw. Smooth the cut edges of the MDF with sandpaper and remove any dust. Cut a 47 x 31½-in. (119 x 80-cm) rectangle of fabric for the headboard front and a 43 x 28-in. (110 x 70-cm) rectangle of fabric for the headboard back.

The rosettes are simple to make and add an elegant finishing touch to the headboard.

2 Drill a hole at each of the three marked points for the buttons. Place the headboard on the batting, draw around it, and cut it to fit. Glue the batting to the front of the board with high-tack craft adhesive.

3 Place the headboard padded side down on the wrong side of the rectangle of fabric for the front of the headboard, so that an even amount of fabric extends beyond the board on all sides. Cut the fabric 4 in. (10 cm) larger all around than the board, following the shape of the board. Starting at the bottom edge, turn the fabric over to the back of the board and staple it in place.

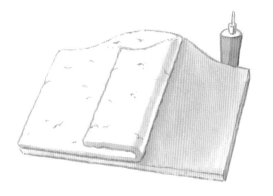

4 Pull the fabric taut and staple it along the top of the headboard, snipping the fabric where necessary to shape the curves. Pull the fabric over the side edges and staple them in the same way, folding in the corners to get a neat finish. Push a bradawl through each of the three holes from the back of the board through the fabric to the front to mark the positions for the buttons.

5 Lay the rectangle of fabric for the back of the board right side down and place the board over it. Draw around the board to mark the shape on the fabric, then remove the board and cut the fabric 1½ in. (4 cm) smaller all around. Turn under and press a ¾-in. (2-cm) hem on all edges, snipping the fabric where necessary to shape the curves. Place the wrong side of the fabric on the back of the board, leaving an even border all the way around, and staple it in place.

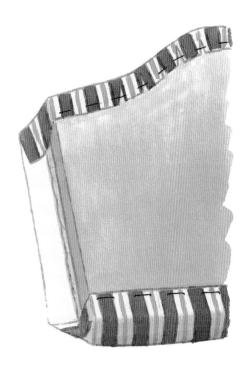

6 Cut the grosgrain ribbon into three equal lengths. Using running stitches, gather each piece along one long edge and sew the short ends together to make a rosette. Finish with a few stitches to secure. Cover the three 1⅛-in. (3-cm) buttons with scraps of fabric following the manufacturer's instructions.

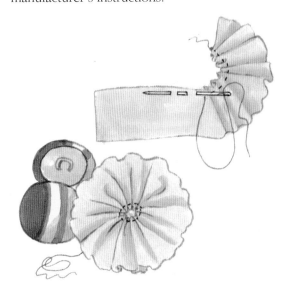

7 Make a few stitches through a plain button on the headboard back, then push the needle and thread through one of the holes from the back to the front. Thread the needle through a rosette and covered button and pull it tightly back through the same hole to the back of the board. Wind the thread around the button on the back several times and secure the thread with a few stitches. Sew on the other two rosettes and covered buttons in the same way.

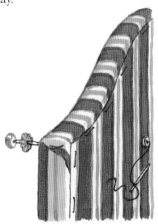

8 Cut the wood studs into two equal lengths and space them evenly approximately 10 in. (25 cm) in from each side edge, with 8 in. (20 cm) of each stud lying flat on the board and the remainder extending beyond the lower edge. Drill two evenly spaced holes through the studs into the MDF and screw them in place.

Professional's Tip: Large Projects

When you're handling large pieces of fabric, not to mention pieces of wood and carpentry tools, you need a good, stable working surface. A large worktable with folding legs will make the job easier (and save your back) and can be stowed away when not needed.

■ A couple of weights will hold fabric in place when cutting, measuring, and joining pieces. You can make your own by covering a small brick with upholstery fabric or thick felt. Just wrap the brick as you would a present, joining the overlapped edges with high-tack fabric glue; then staple the fabric at each end.

Padded headboard cover

This softly padded cover fits over an existing wooden headboard and is held in place with ties at the side. The headboard must have a straight top edge in order for the cover to sit flat. The cover can be made to fit any size of headboard. For large beds, you may need to join pieces of fabric in order to reach the required width. If this is the case, use a full-width panel of fabric in the center and join a narrower matching piece to each side. Choose a fabric to coordinate with your bed linen.

You Will Need

- 1¼ yd. (1 m) of 54-in. (137-cm)-wide cotton upholstery fabric (add more to center a larger pattern repeat)
- 1½ yd. (1.2 m) of 54-in. (137-cm)-wide cotton lining
- 37¼ x 38¼ in. (94 x 97-cm) 8-oz. (250-g) piece of polyester batting
- 2¼ yd. (2 m) piping cord
- matching polycotton thread

Note: The headboard measures 36 x 37 in. (91 x 94 cm).

Cutting Out

Note: Seam allowances of ⅝ in. (1.5 cm) are included throughout unless otherwise stated.

From the upholstery fabric, cut a 37¼ x 20½-in. (94 x 52-cm) rectangle for the headboard front, a 37¼ x 19¼-in. (94 x 48-cm) rectangle for the headboard back, and eight 12 x 3½-in. (30 x 9-cm) strips for the ties.

From the lining fabric cut one 37¼ x 38¼-in. (94 x 97-cm) rectangle and two 26 x 13-in. (67 x 33-cm) rectangles for the side flaps.

Make 2¼ yd. (2 m) of piping from the lining fabric (see page 155).

1 Fold one of the tie strips in half lengthwise, right sides together, and machine stitch down the long edge and along one short edge. Trim the seam, clip the corners, and turn the tie right side out. Press the tie flat, with the seam along a side edge. Make seven more ties in the same way.

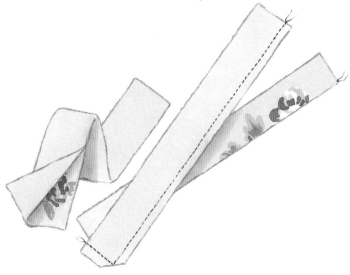

3 HOURS OR LESS

LOW-SEW PROJECT

Floral or other busy fabrics benefit from a plain treatment.

143

2 Fold one of the side-flap pieces in half widthwise, right sides together. Stitch along both side edges, leaving the edge opposite the fold open. Trim the seam, turn the flap right side out, and press. Make the second side flap in the same way.

3 Right sides together, pin the front and back rectangles together along the top edge, and machine stitch. Press open the seam.

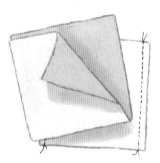

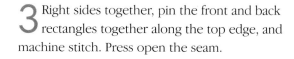
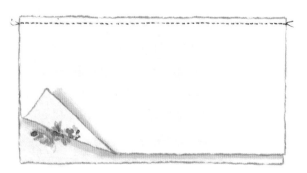

4 With the right side facing you, mark the halfway point on each side edge with a pin. Pin and then baste a length of piping along each side edge, with the raw edges facing outward and the piping just inside the seam allowance. Measure 3½ in. (9 cm) from the central pin markers in each direction and pin ties in corresponding pairs on each side, with the raw edges together and the ties facing inward.

5 Pin two more pairs of ties in place, leaving 3½ in. (9 cm) between them and the first set, and baste to secure.

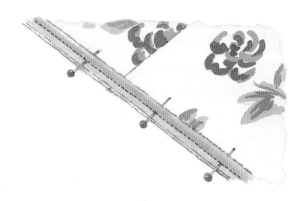

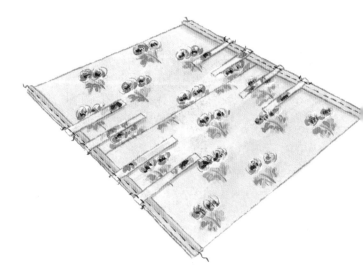

6 Pin a flap to each back side edge, with the top edge of the flap ⅛ in. (½ cm) above the seam that joins the front and back pieces, covering two ties, and raw edges facing outward. Baste in place. Place the lining on top of the main piece, right sides together.

7 Place the batting on top of the lining and baste all the layers together. Machine stitch around all four sides, leaving an 18-in. (45-cm) opening along the bottom edge of the back. Trim the seams, clip the corners, and turn the headboard cover right side out. Slipstitch the opening closed and press lightly.

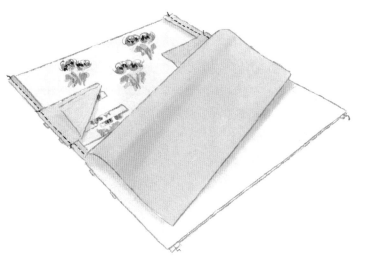

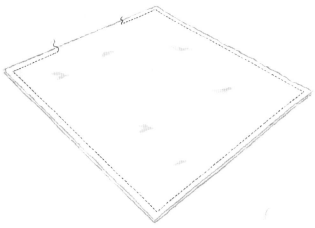

Professional's Tip: Pressing

For a professional finish, make good pressing techniques a priority. Use a press cloth—a piece of cotton lawn or similar—between iron and fabric when pressing on the right side, to avoid leaving a shine on the fabric.

■ When pressing a seam, first press it flat, without opening it, on both sides, to embed the stitches. Use an up-and-down motion when pressing; don't slide the iron back and forth.

■ Next, open the seam, running your thumbnail or the point of the iron along the stitching. Finally, press the opened seam flat.

■ If the seam is to lie on an edge, as for these ties, carefully work it into place with your fingers after turning the tie right side out. If necessary, hold it in place with basting stitches (not too tight). Use a press cloth and steam—and take your time!

Techniques

Essential sewing equipment

Sewing machine

A good sewing machine should give years of reliable service and be able to stitch all the soft furnishings for your home that you could possibly need. Modern machines are capable of all kinds of automated tasks, but many stitchers never make use of the vast array of stitch patterns that their machines can produce. Unless you intend to do machine embroidery and experiment with a huge selection of fancy stitches, you will probably not need anything so complex or sophisticated.

If you buy a secondhand machine, make sure that the manufacturer is still in business so that spare parts are available if any need replacing.

Sewing machine features

When choosing a basic machine, look for the features that you really intend to use. Try out the machine to check how easily the tension and stitch length can be adjusted and how neatly a zigzag stitch can be worked for making buttonholes, finishing edges or covering edges for appliqué.

The basic foot that comes with the machine is fine for most jobs. You will also need a piping or zipper foot (generally supplied with the machine) for sewing piping or bulky braid into seams. The foot plate is usually marked to provide guide marks for different widths of seam. If it isn't, place a strip of masking tape on the plate as a guide line so that your seams will be straight and consistent in width.

Care of your sewing machine

Remember to clean your machine regularly. Use a small brush to remove any lint, stray threads, broken pins, and machine needle splinters that might have accumulated under the foot plate. Oil the machine following the manufacturer's maintenance instructions. Change the needle regularly and use one that suits the weight of fabric you are sewing.

Scissors

There are several types of scissors. Use the right one for your purposes:

Dressmaker's scissors have long blades and, if you want to ensure that the blades stay really sharp, they should only be used for cutting fabric. The handles are shaped at an angle so that they cut accurately.

Sewing scissors are smaller than dressmaker's scissors, and have straight handles. They can be used to trim corners and seams and to make small notches in curved seams. Keep them next to the sewing machine so that you have them at hand for cutting the thread after you have stitched and finished a seam.

Embroidery scissors are small, with short sharp-pointed ends. They are useful for trimming intricate things and for snipping into tight corners.

Paper scissors should only be used for cutting out pattern pieces and templates from paper, cardstock, or cardboard. Do not use your dressmaker's or sewing scissors for cutting these, as they will quickly become blunted.

Needles

Hand sewing needles come in different sizes to suit different purposes.

Sharps are best for general-purpose jobs and can be found in various lengths—medium to long for basting, and short for slip stitching.

Machine needles need to be suited to the type of fabric you are sewing. A 12/80 or 14/90 sized needle is suitable for most jobs; for a lightweight fabric, choose a finer needle such as a 10/70.

Thimble

It can take a while to get used to using a thimble— but once you've got the hang of it, you won't want to sew without one. A thimble protects your fingertip from needle pricks and provides a firm surface to push behind the needle when sewing heavy fabrics.

Dressmaker's pins

There are lots of different types of pins available, in different lengths and thicknesses. Glass-headed pins are easy to see and catch with your nails. Make sure that they are made from glass rather than plastic, which will melt under a hot iron. Longer thin pins are used for finer fabrics.

When you're buying pins, choose ones that are made from rustless steel so that you don't run the risk of marking your fabric.

Threads

If you are unable to find an exact color match, choose a thread that is slightly darker than your fabric. Sewing threads come in natural and synthetic fibers, so choose one that matches the fiber of your fabric. Mercerized cotton can be used for cotton and linen.

For basting, you can use any waste thread or basting thread, which is designed specifically for this purpose. Basting thread is not mercerized, so it snaps easily and is easy to remove.

Marking tools

It is useful to have marking tools that will not leave any permanent marks on the fabric.

Tailor's chalk and chalk pencils, which can be sharpened to give a finer point, can be brushed off. Try to choose a color that is close to your fabric color but will still show.

Dressmaker's pens leave a water-soluble mark that can be washed out; some are light sensitive, so the marks will fade away completely.

Dressmaker's carbon paper can be used to mark seamlines or to copy embroidery designs. It is usually used with a sharp pencil or a spiked wheel to transfer lines of small dots.

Iron

For a really neat and professional finish, always press seams and hems as you go so that the edges are sharp and defined. Take care to set your iron to the temperature recommended for your fabric. A steam iron is excellent for use on natural fabrics. Discharge the first burst of steam on a waste piece of fabric to be sure that no sediment will stain the fabric, and keep the base plate clean to prevent marks. A well padded ironing board, the larger the better, also makes the job a whole lot easier.

Tape measure

Always keep a tape measure at hand, as well as a ruler and set square for pattern making.

Preparing and cutting fabrics

Preparing fabrics

Always wash your fabric before you begin a sewing project, so that any shrinkage will occur before you cut out the fabric. If you are a beginner, start by using woven checked and striped fabrics, as it is easy to follow the grain and you can follow the pattern to cut straight lines. The edges of the fabric are woven a little tighter than the rest, so always remove or snip the selvages at regular intervals to release this tightness.

Cutting out

In order for your home furnishing projects to withstand lots of wear and tear, you need to know how the grain of the fabric runs. Fabrics that are cut out following the grain will be more hard-wearing and keep their shape better. The exception to this is bias strips, which need to have

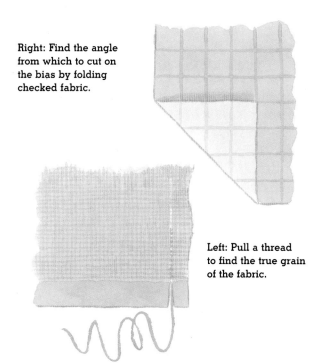

Right: Find the angle from which to cut on the bias by folding checked fabric.

Left: Pull a thread to find the true grain of the fabric.

a certain amount of stretch to maneuver around corners and curves.

On good-quality patterned fabrics the print follows the grain, so you can cut along the pattern. Where a print is placed slightly off the grain you will need to cut it following the pattern, so that pieces of fabric such as curtains will match. If the pattern is too far off the grain, however, return the fabric to the store as it will be inferior in quality.

Using a rotary cutter

When cutting out lots of same-sized straight-sided fabric pieces for patchwork, using a rotary cutter can speed things up and give precise results, as it allows you to cut through several layers at a time. It is a good way of cutting strips of fabric that can then be cut into smaller rectangles, squares, and

Right: To cut with a rotary cutter, hold the ruler over the area that you want to end up with, and run the cutter along the edge, cutting away from you.

triangles. The blade should be really sharp with a safety cover as a precaution.

Cutting mat

The cutter also needs a self-healing cutting mat to protect the tabletop and a rotary ruler, made of thick clear plastic with straight lines and angles, to follow with the cutter.

Simple sewing

Sewing machine tension

Once the tension on your machine is correct, there is hardly any need to alter it—but different fabric weights and a machine's quirky behavior can sometimes call for some adjustment. You need to achieve an even stitch where the top and bobbin threads are working evenly together, linking

together midway through the fabric. A top thread that is too tight or a taut bobbin thread indicates something is amiss and the tension needs attention. Seen here as a seam cross-section,

Correct tension: Seen here as a seam cross-section, the stitch looks the same on both sides of the fabric.

Bottom thread is too tight: Seen here in cross-section, the bottom thread lies in a line and the top thread shows through on the back of the seam.

Top thread is too tight: Seen here in cross-section, the top thread lies in a line and the bobbin thread is visible in the seam.

Basic hand stitches

Even when you are making things using a sewing machine, there are always times when you are called upon to do a few hand stitches.

Basting stitch

Pins are often enough to hold fabrics together ready for sewing, but sometimes you will need to baste the layers together with long stitches for neatness and extra security. Basting stitch is a temporary stitch used to hold the fabric securely

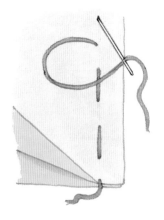

in position; after stitching, the basting is removed. Use waste thread and a long needle to make long, even straight stitches.

Slip stitch
Slip stitches are used to close an opening in a side seam or finish off a hem. Slide the needle through the folded edge, then back through the lower fabric, catching just a few threads of the fabric at a time. The stitches should be small and evenly

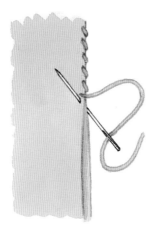

spaced. When done properly, the stitching should be almost invisible from both sides.

Buttonhole stitch
Buttonholes are usually done by machine, but they can be worked by hand. Buttonhole stitch is a strong, hard-wearing stitch that binds the fabric's raw edges. This stitch can also be used to secure rings and hooks to curtain headings and fabric.

Insert the needle upward through the fabric at the required distance from the fabric edge and twist the loop of thread around the needle point.

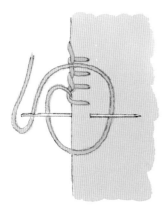

Pull the needle through to form a neat, knotted edging over the raw edge. Make consecutive stitches close together in the same way, so that the stitches form a narrow, continuous band concealing the fabric beneath.

Hem stitch
Slip stitches are used to secure a hem but can be worked in a slightly more spaced-out formation to secure a hem more quickly. Bring the needle from the folded edge and catch a few threads of the

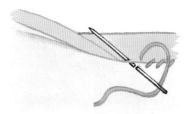

main fabric, then slip the needle back into the folded edge and run it through the fold for a short distance.

Seams and hems

Plain seam
Use the markers on the base plate of the sewing machine to keep seamlines straight and consistent. Seams are generally made so that the edges will be inside the piece, out of sight. To do this, place the fabrics with right sides together, and pin them at regular intervals. Pins can be placed following the seamline (in which case you must remove them before the machine needle has the chance to run into them) or pinned at right angles to the seamline. You will still need to take care as the machine foot goes over them, but the needle is much less likely to hit a pin.

When stitching seams with pleats or gathers, always baste the layers together first.

Several of the projects in this book join fabrics so that the seams are on the right side, but the seams are then covered with lengths of ribbon that are top stitched in place.

Finishing seams

Seams need to be finished so that they don't ravel and will stand up to wash and wear. Work a machine zigzag stitch along the raw edges or, for a really professional finish, use an overlocker if you are lucky enough to have one. Fabric edges can also be cut with pinking shears to keep them neat.

Turning a corner

When the machine has to turn a corner, sew up to the seam allowance of the next side, leaving the needle in the fabric. Lift the machine foot and pivot from the needle point through 90 degrees to position the foot for the next side. Lower the foot and continue to sew. Clip off the corners to within ⅛ in. (3 mm) of the stitching before turning the fabric to the right side so that the corner isn't too bulky.

Double hem

A double hem is turned twice, the first turning being narrower than the second. Press under the folds, pin, then baste in place. The hem can then be machine stitched close to the inside fold or slip stitched by hand if you don't want the stitching to show.

Mitering hemmed corners

When two hems meet at a corner (for example, on a curtain), mitering will give a professional finish and stop corners from becoming too bulky. The fabric is folded over to meet at the corner so that the seam line is exactly midway between both side edges and makes a 45° angle.

1. Fold in a hem of equal depth on both sides of the fabric, and press. Unfold the turnings, then fold in the corner to make a triangle that crosses where the side fold lines meet at the corner, and press.

2. Fold the corner right sides together, so that the raw edges and creases meet. Pin and stitch along the pressed diagonal line.

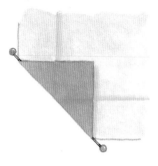

3. Trim to within ¼ in. (6 mm) of the seam, and press the seam open. Turn to the right side and press flat. Hem the side edges in place. Slip stitch the miter.

Closures

Inserting a zipper

A zipper makes it easy to remove pillow covers for laundering. It needs to be placed close to an edge or set into a seam so that it is not immediately obvious.

1. With right sides together, pin the fabrics together. Use pin markers to mark a space at the center which is the same length as the zipper (measuring from just outside the stoppers). Stitch from each end up to marked points, leaving an opening between the markers. Now machine baste the opening. Press the seam open.

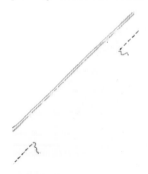

2. Place the zipper in the opening from underneath and pin, then hand baste it in place with the zipper closed.

3. Using the zipper foot, machine topstitch the zipper from the right side, an equal distance away

from the zipper down both sides and across both ends. Remove the hand and machine basting. Open the zipper.

Inserting a zipper into a piped seam

1. Pipe one edge of the seam, but do not close the opening. Open the zipper and place it face down on the piped seam, with the teeth in line with the piping stitching. Baste the zipper in place, then stitch along the seam ⅛ in. (3 mm) from the teeth.

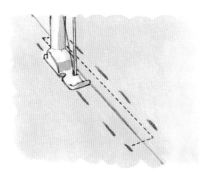

2. Turn back the seam allowance so that the piping lies at the edge of the opening. Close the zipper. Press under the seam allowance of the other piece of fabric.

3. Bring the folded edge over the zipper so that it meets the piping. Baste the length of the seam through all thicknesses and then machine stitch ¼ in. (6 mm) from the folded edge and across the ends of the zipper up to the piping. Remove the basting stitches.

Making buttonholes by hand

1. Draw both outer edges of the buttonhole lightly in pencil and join the two lines at the ends to make a rectangle. Work small running or back stitches along the lines all around the edge.

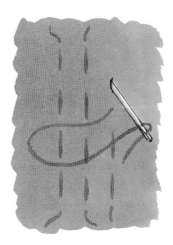

2. Using sharp embroidery scissors, cut a slit down the center of the buttonhole. Following the instructions on page 149, work buttonhole stitch along both sides of the slit, taking the stitches to just beyond the running or back stitches so that the sides are even.

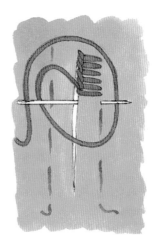

3. Work radiating stitches to turn the top edge or make a bar tack of several stitches the width of the buttonhole at each end.

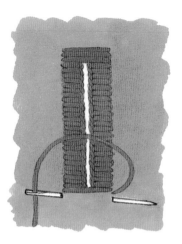

Making buttonholes by machine

Different machines use slightly different methods for making buttonholes, so always check the instructions supplied with your machine.

A machine-made buttonhole is generally made by working two closely worked lines of zigzag stitching side by side, with a bar basted block at each end holding it together.

The line made between the zigzag lines then needs to be slit open using a seam ripper or embroidery scissors.

1. Mark the center and length of the buttonhole with chalk or a light pencil line, and baste along the line.

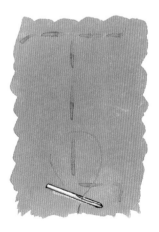

2. Set the machine to work a very closely spaced zigzag stitch. Run a line of machine stitching above and below the basted center line. Work satin stitches along the top row.

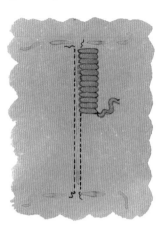

3. Take several long stitches at both ends. Work satin stitch along the bottom row. Cut the slit.

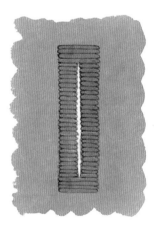

Stitching on buttons

1. Stitching on a button with two holes.

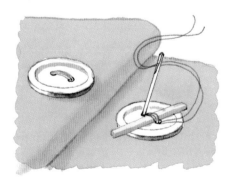

2. Stitching on a button with four holes—known as crossways pattern.

3. Stitching on a button with a shank.

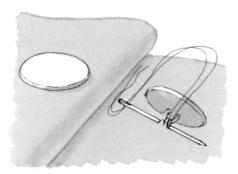

Covering buttons

Buttons to cover (in covered button kits) are usually made of plastic or preformed metal and covered in one of two ways. For both, you will need to cut out a circle of fabric to cover the mold. The packaging usually includes a template, which shows the size that the circle needs to be.

For the first type of mold, you need to make small running stitches around the edge of the circle, and then pull the stitches so that the circle gathers around the edges. Place the mold inside the circle, pull the stitches to completely enclose it, and make a few stitches to hold the thread secure. The back of the button mold will then either pop in place or prongs will push up from the mold beneath which you need to bend flat against the fabric.

The second type has a serrated edging. Simply fold the circle of fabric over the mold (it will be held in place on the sharp edges),then place a button back in position to enclose the edges of the fabric.

Decorative trims

There is a vast choice of notions, trimmings, tassels, and fringes available for embellishing home furnishings. Simple fabric binding, piping, lace trim, rick-rack braid, fringing, and beaded trims are just a few of the options open to you. You can also make your own decorative tassels (see page 93).

If you use a trim such as beaded trim or other hard, breakable trim, it's a good idea to put tissue paper around it before you attempt to stitch it to the edge of your project as this protects it from the metal plate of the sewing machine and stops it from making a noise as you sew.

Binding

A fabric binding is perhaps the most commonly used form of decorative trim. It gives a neat, professional-looking finish to pillows and covers, without making a strong style statement in its own right. You can use matching or coordinating fabrics to bind edges. Alternatively, you can pick out a color from a patterned fabric to make more of a feature of it.

Straight edges (square pillows, for example) can be bound with strips cut on the grain.

Binding for a curved edge must be cut on the bias; this makes it slightly stretchy, which allows you to set piping along curved edges. You will need to clip the seam allowance now and then to help the piping follow the curves.

Piping cord can be covered in binding to give a clearly defined, but still soft edge. Alternatively you can use a ready-made, store-bought piping or cord edging to achieve the same effect. Piping cord is available in different sizes, so it can be as fine or as chunky as you like. When you cut strips of fabric to cover piping cord, the part that will be sewn into the seam should be the same depth as the seam allowance once the piping has been folded and stitched around the cord.

Making bias binding

1. Cut strips of fabric (following the grain if you are binding straight edges, and on the bias for curved edges) so that, when they are joined, they will make up the length you require.

2. For a continuous strip, cut out a rectangle that is at least twice as long as it is wide. With the short edges at top and bottom, fold the top right-hand corner over so that the top edge runs down the

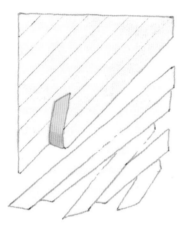

left-hand side edge of the rectangle to make a right-angled triangle. Press the fold and cut off the triangle along the fold line. With right sides together, stitch the top straight edge of the triangle to the opposite short edge of the rectangle, using a ¼-in. (6-mm) seam; press the seam open. Mark lines across the fabric the width of the strips you require and parallel to the slanted ends. Number the rows, staggering the numbers so that the first row on the left is 1, the first row on the right is 2, the second row on the left is 2, and so on. Fold the piece with right sides together and, matching the numbers (2 to 2, 3 to 3, and so on), stitch to make a tube. Press the seam open. Turn to the right side and, starting from the top, cut along the ruled lines to make a continuous strip.

3. To join strips to make a continuous length, pin two short edges with right sides together along the straight grain, as shown.

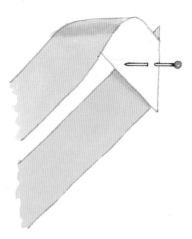

4. Stitch the seam and press it open, trimming away the pointed ends.

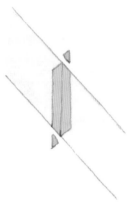

5. If the tape is for binding rather than piping, fold both long edges to the center and press in place. Fold and press the strip lengthwise down the center.

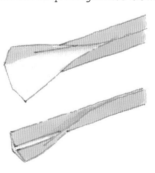

Making binding using a tape maker

A tape maker is a handy little gadget that speeds up the process of making binding considerably. Cut the binding to the required length and width, as described opposite, joining lengths together if necessary. Push the binding through the wide end of the tape maker, with the wrong side of the material facing up. Pin the binding down and pull the tape maker along, ironing the binding as you go. The sides will automatically be folded over. Open out the binding and follow the fold lines when stitching.

Applying binding

Binding can be stitched to the right side of the item you are making, and then turned over to the wrong side as explained below. Alternatively, it can be stitched to the wrong side and folded over to the right side. The first method is more suited to slip stitching by hand, while the second means that you can topstitch the binding in place from the right side, which will give a tidier finish when working by machine.

1. With right sides together, pin one edge of the binding to the raw edge of the fabric.

2. Stitch along the fold line, removing pins as you go. Cut notches in the seam allowance here and there to follow any curves.

3. Fold the binding to the wrong side of the piece, press under a hem along the raw bias edge if it is not already pressed, and pin in place so the folded edge just overlaps the stitching. Stitch close to the folded edge on the machine or slip stitch by hand.

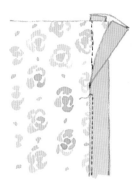

Making piping

1. Make a bias strip as for binding, but without pre-folding it. With wrong sides together and the piping cord sandwiched in the middle, fold the strip in half lengthwise. With a piping foot, stitch close to the cord.

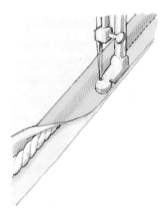

2. With the raw edges facing outward and the cord inside and following the seam allowance, pin the piping to the right side of the piece along the edge. Clip the seam allowance on curves or corners. Baste in place.

3. Where two ends of piping meet, join them by opening out the piping for a short distance and then twisting the ends of the cord together. With right sides together, stitch the strips together where they meet, trim off any excess, and press the seam flat. Fold back over the joined cord ends and sew close to the cord to enclose it.

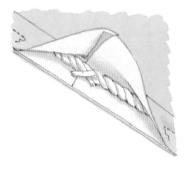

4. Place the other fabric on top, right side down, if using. Machine stitch the seam, stitching close to the cord.

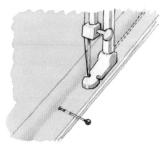

Stitching on other kinds of decorative trim

Other braids and trimmings can be stitched into seams in the same way as piping. If the trimming is bulky, you will again need to use a zipper or piping foot to stitch alongside the trimming. Trimmings with an attractive band along one edge can also be stitched on by hand after the item has been made up, using a slip stitch to hold the trimming securely in place.

1. Pin the trimming in place on the right side of the main piece and baste.

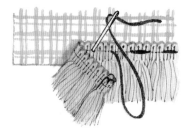

2. Machine stitch on the right side of the item—or slip stitch by hand if you want the join to be invisible.

Ribbon and braid are useful decorative devices for soft furnishings as well as for covering up seams and raw edges. Pin and baste the ribbon in place and topstitch on the right side, stitching close to both edges of the ribbon.

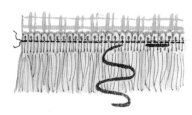

Curtains

Curtains are such a huge subject that people have written whole books on them. For quick-and-easy projects, such as the ones in this book, here are the more important guidelines.

Measuring

When measuring for your curtains, you need to know exactly where the top of the curtain will be in relation to the window to which it will be attached, so you need to fix the rod or pole in position first.

Curtain hardware

Drapery rods are an unobtrusive, flat band with rings that slide underneath along the bottom edge. The top edge of the curtain is usually above the rod, so that the rod will be hidden when the curtains are closed. Rods can be fitted above the window, or within or outside of a recessed window, and can follow the shape of a bay window.

Curtain poles are usually meant to be seen above the curtain. The curtain is attached by means of either tab tops on the curtains, which are tied or looped over the pole, or hooks on the curtain heading tape, which slot into the rings that slide along the pole. The heading tape needs to be positioned so that the curtain will end just below the ring. A pole can be fitted above the window frame, with a decorative finial at each end, or set inside a recessed window by means of special brackets at each side.

How long should your curtain be?

Decide whether your curtains will look best at sill or floor length or somewhere in between. You may even want to make them a little longer than floor length, so that the bottom edge will puddle into folds on the floor. Measure the length from the top of the rod or from just underneath the pole.

How much fabric do you need?

The number of fabric widths needed to cover a window is determined by the length of the rod or pole and the style of the curtain heading you choose. Some headings require a lot of fabric and others much less. Shown opposite and on page

158 are four of the most popular types of heading tape; for each one, we specify how many times the width of the curtain rod you need to allow for to create the appropriate degree of fullness.

Number of widths

To calculate the total number of widths required, multiply the fabric fullness by the rod or pole width. Divide this amount by a single fabric width and round it up to the nearest whole number. For pairs of curtains, halve this amount to get the number of widths that have to be joined to make one curtain. Attach any half-widths to the outside edge of each curtain. Make up as a matching pair.

Curtain lengths

Multiply the curtain length by the number of fabric widths needed and add extra for turnings at the top and bottom hemmed edges. After the first length of fabric, add the depth of the pattern repeat to each subsequent length—for example, when using a fabric with a 14-in. (35-cm) repeat for a curtain that requires four lengths of fabric, you will need to add 14 in. (35 cm) x 3 to the total amount. Manufacturers will tell you exactly how big the pattern repeat of your chosen fabric is. On small-checked patterns and weaves it will be hardly noticeable, but for larger patterns it can add a lot of extra fabric and additional expense.

Lining fabric—you will need the same amount as for the main fabric, but there is no need to allow for pattern repeats. Lining fabrics can be bought in the same widths as home decorating fabrics, so buy the width that matches your curtain fabric.

Heading tapes

A heading tape is designed to take up the fullness of the curtain fabric in even gathers or pleats and provide a means by which the curtain can be hung from a rod or pole. If the curtain doesn't have a valance or pelmet, the heading will be an important feature. There are several styles to choose from and your choice will be based on the look you want to achieve, the weight of the curtain, and your own personal tastes.

The cords that run along the tape need to be knotted at each end, pulled from the outside edge of the curtain, and then knotted when the amount of pleating or gathering is achieved. Never cut off the excess cord, as it will need to be released for laundering.

Different tapes require different widths of fabric to look at their best.

Shirred heading

Shirred heading tape gives an evenly gathered heading for lighter-weight curtains such as unlined kitchen curtains. It is made of cotton or a synthetic fiber and works particularly well with sheers and lightweight fabrics. When using shirred heading tape, you should allow 1½ times the rod width—or up to 3 widths for sheers.

Pencil-pleat heading

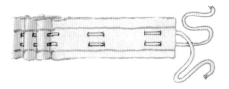

A pencil-pleat heading gives a deep, evenly gathered heading and is suited to all weights of curtains, whether lined or unlined. It has two rows of pockets running across the back for attaching the hook to. If you want the curtain to cover the rod, then fix the hooks to the bottom row; if you want the curtain to hang below the rod, use the top row. When using pencil-pleat heading tape, you should allow 2¼ to 2½ times the rod width.

Triple-pleat heading

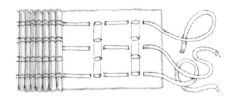

Triple-pleat heading tape gives pronounced pleats with three edges, with evenly spaced gaps in between. It is suitable for heavier curtain styles, lined and possibly interlined. You may need to pull the cords to pleat the tape in order to understand how the formation works, as the pleats need to be evenly spaced along the top of the curtain with a flat area at either end. This style needs a two-pronged hook, one for each pleat, which will be threaded through pockets at the base of each pleat to cover the rod. A few hand stitches across the base of the front of each pleat keep the pleats tight. When using triple-pleat heading tape, you should allow approximately 2 times the track width.

Cylindrical and goblet-pleat heading

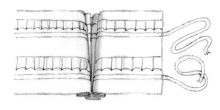

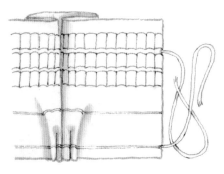

Cylindrical and goblet-pleat heading tape gives a pronounced tube effect. Each pleat can be stuffed with rolled-up tissue paper for extra pleat definition. When using either of these heading tapes, you should allow approximately 2 to 2¼ times the rod width.

Slipcovers

Slipcovers look most professional when the fit is accurate and the seams follow the lines of the chair beneath, without any baggy or loose areas. If you're a complete beginner, start off with simple seat covers and unstructured slipcovers before you embark on projects that have a more tailored finish and piped edges.

It is worth making covers up in muslin first before you cut the pieces out of expensive fabric. This gives you the opportunity to try the cover on your seat and to make any slight adjustments to get the fit right. It also makes it easier to calculate how much fabric you will need, as you can lay the pieces on an old sheet folded to the width of your fabric following the grain and easily measure exactly how much will be required. Remember to take the pattern on your fabric into consideration and to match or center motifs on the pieces where necessary.

For a precise fit, pin the fabric pieces wrong side out to the chair you are covering and pin the pieces together along the seams. There needs to be a small amount of ease so the cover will slip over or off the chair for laundering.

Index

Suppliers

In the United States

Calico Corners
203 Gale Lane
Kennett Square, PA 19048
1-800-213-6366
Monday–Friday 9 a.m. to 5 p.m. EST
www.calicocorners.com

Decorator fabrics and upholstery materials

Coats & Clark
Consumer Services
P.O. Box 12229
Greenville, SC 29612-0229
1-800-648-1479
www.coatsandclark.com

Sewing, knitting, and craft products

Jo-Ann Fabric
2361 Rosecrans Avenue
Suite 360
El Segundo, CA 90245
1-800-525-4951
Monday–Friday 9 a.m. to 6 p.m. EST
www.joann.com

Sewing supplies and fabrics

In Canada

bb bargoons
2784 Yonge St
Toronto, ON M4N 2J2
416-481-5273
www.bbbargoons.com

C & M Textiles
7500 Saint-Hubert
Montreal, QC H2R 2N6
514-272-0247

Fabricland/Fabricville
Over 170 stores from coast to coast
in Canada
For a complete store listing see
www.fabricville.com
or
www.fabricland.com

Fanny's Fabrics
Over 30 stores in Western Canada
For a complete store listing see
http://profile.canadianretail.com/fannys
#about